WYNDHAM AND CHILDREN FIRST

Wyndham
and Children First

LORD EGREMONT

MACMILLAN
London · Melbourne · Toronto
1968

© *Egremont & Hutchinson Ltd* 1968

First published 1968
Reprinted 1968
MACMILLAN AND CO LTD
Little Essex Street London W C 2
and also at Bombay Calcutta and Madras
Macmillan South Africa (Publishers) Pty Ltd Johannesburg
The Macmillan Company of Australia Pty Ltd Melbourne
The Macmillan Company of Canada Ltd Toronto

Printed in Great Britain by
ROBERT MACLEHOSE AND CO LTD
The University Press, Glasgow

Contents

Illustrations

The author and publishers wish to thank those who have kindly given permission for the photographs to be reproduced as follows : 7, British Museum; 18, Camera Press; 13, *Country Life*; 1, 2, 3, 4, 8, 9, Courtauld Institute of Art; 11, 12, G. G. Garland; 6, National Gallery; 15, 20, Ivor Nicholas; 5, Photo Precision; 16, Thomson Newspapers.

Pictures 1, 5, 6, are in the Petworth Collection; and 2, 3, 4, 8, 9, are in the author's private collection.

Salute

TO GEORGE HUTCHINSON, C.B.E.
AND OTHER FRIENDS

For this book I am indebted, most of all, to my friend George Hutchinson. But for me, it would not have been written : but for him, it wouldn't have been written either. Ever since he first suggested the book he has prodded, pushed, provoked and goaded me into writing it. He is no mean writer himself. I have known him a good number of years, first as one of the most distinguished of the political correspondents, when he was with the *Evening Standard*, then when he was directing Conservative Party publicity, and latterly as the managing director of the *Spectator*, – in which I have been very happy to appear as a fellow contributor. Now he has edited these memoirs.

When he first spoke about them to Mr Harold Macmillan, my old master was pleased – for me. 'Just the sort of exercise that John needs,' said Mr Macmillan. Well, I hope that I have not disappointed him, and I owe Mr Macmillan affectionate thanks for much encouragement and help.

I also wish to thank Lord Crawford and Balcarres, Sir Leslie Farrer and Mr Patrick Hancock; and, for permission to quote copyright material, Christabel Lady Aberconway and Messrs Hutchinson (*A Wiser Woman*), Mr Robert

Murphy and Messrs Collins (*A Diplomat Among Warriors*), Lady Diana Cooper (*Trumpets from the Steep*) and Lord Norwich (a sonnet by Duff Cooper). I am grateful, too, to Sir Michael Fraser, Mr Norman Collins, Mr J. W. M. Thompson, Mr David Rees and Mr Osbert Lancaster. In one way or another they have all given me their kind help.

My thanks are also due to Miss Delia Bateman, who was such a patient secretary during the preparation of the book.

E.

Petworth House

Prelude

ON the evening of 4 June 1920 my parents gave a dinner-party at Windsor, where they had a house because the Life Guards, whom my father was commanding, were in barracks there. After dinner everybody except my mother went off to Eton to watch the fireworks. My mother decided to stay at home; which was wise, because I was born that night.

I cannot remember much about the Life Guards except that I would have liked to join them and once as a child was taken to see them at Hyde Park Barracks. A detachment of the regiment came clattering in on their horses from some ceremonial duty. A kindly Corporal of Horse explained to my nurse and me what would happen next: an officer would give the command, 'Prepare to dismount; dismount.' On this occasion, however, the officer must have been displeased with his men, for what he said was 'Climb down, you bloody monkeys.'

Most of my childhood I spent at Edmondthorpe Hall, my father's home in Leicestershire, a nice house, quite large, with sizeable stables adjoining it. There I was brought up with my sister Ursula and my brothers Henry and Mark.

Looking back, I see it now as a distinctly Edwardian set-up, though it persisted well into the second quarter of the century. We had a quantity of servants, many of them related to each other. There was the Harrison family, consisting of Aggie the cook, Alice the head housemaid, Ada, my nanny, whom we called Nan, and a fourth sister, Nelly, a nursery-maid. There was another nursery-maid called Nancy. The butler was Mr Green. The stud groom, Mr Hall, presided over the stables. His three sons, Syd, Stan and Bert, worked with him in the stables, and in the hunting season were helped by a contingent of strappers. Then there was Mr Jackson, the chauffeur, and his cars. Mr Hall used to complain that Mr Jackson, because of his mechanical skill, was paid more than he was. Mr Hall used to say to us children, with inspissated contempt for Mr Jackson, 'Whenever one of Jackson's cars goes wrong, he sends it into a garage. Whenever one of my horses goes wrong, I sit up with it all night.'

My memory must be exaggerating, but it seems to me now that scarcely a year went by without one of the maids becoming pregnant. Whenever this happened, the girl's condition would be reported to my mother by Aggie or Alice or somebody. A one-woman rescue party – my mother – would then set out. She was pretty and tough. I remember once going with her to see the parents of an errant maid. The maid's mother, in tears, said that she would never again open her door to the wicked girl. At this, my mother spoke up sternly, reminding her that a daughter was always a daughter.

Both my parents were very fond of hunting. My mother looked exceptionally fine on a horse and always rode side-saddle. Side-saddle is very pretty and all that, and helps to keep you on the horse. But should the horse fall, you are unlikely to fall free, and so you are liable to suffer damage. This happened to my mother several times. My father told me that if I got married and had a daughter, I should make sure that my wife and daughter rode astride. This I have done.

To all of us as children my father was kind but distant. Family life is all right for those who can stand it. He could barely stand it, except for his devotion to my mother. As to disciplining his children, the very notion got on his nerves. Whenever I had done anything wrong, and he was pressed by my mother to tell me off, we would have a most embarrassing interview, with him tongue-tied and me sorry. These interviews usually ended with 'Don't do it again. What you have done is almost as bad as shooting a fox.' I can't remember how, but I shouldn't think that any of my offences ever came near to that.

When I was six my parents started to worry about my intellect. My governess had reported that, try as she might, she could not get me to learn even to read. But my nurse said : 'He isn't half-witted : he's half blind.' I was sent to an eye-specialist. From then on, with the aid of a thick pair of spectacles, I pursued my studies with better results.

My father had a good library, and he made me free of it. Reading became one of my great pleasures as a boy at Edmondthorpe, at my preparatory school near Ascot and at Eton. It has remained one of the pleasures of my life, though I seldom read novels. I like memoirs and history – and I have found a lot of enjoyment in my own voluminous archives at Petworth.

Studying the history of Petworth and the people who have lived there has been great fun for me since I came into the estate. Of course I have known the house all my life and used to stay there with my Uncle Charles, the third Lord Leconfield, from whom I inherited my various possessions, territorial and otherwise.

CHAPTER ONE

Earlier Egremonts

THE Manor of Petworth was bequeathed by Henry I to his second wife, Queen Adeliza. She presented it to her brother Joscelyn, who took the name of Percy when he married Lady Agnes de Percy, a great northern heiress. This lady was the great-granddaughter of one William de Percy (nicknamed Algernon, meaning in old French 'with the whiskers'), who had accompanied William of Normandy to England in 1066 and was rewarded with large grants of land in many counties, including those of the Saxon Earl of Northumberland, whose daughter he married. So began in 1150 the Percy connection with Petworth.

In 1377 the Earldom of Northumberland was renewed in favour of the first of those eleven rich and powerful Earls of Northumberland who gained real importance during the three turbulent centuries that followed. Rich, powerful and important though they were, they were however unlucky. No fewer than seven of the eleven were killed in battle, executed, murdered or imprisoned. Another, the 6th Earl, is said to have died of a broken heart; his misfortunes included falling in love with Anne Boleyn at the same time as Henry VIII.

Henry Percy, the 9th Earl, was in many ways the most distinguished of his line. He was a learned man and a patron of learning, and he amassed a fine library of books, many of which are still at Petworth. He, too, was unfortunate in his dealings with higher authority and spent sixteen years in the Tower of London under suspicion of complicity in the Gunpowder Plot (a cousin of his was certainly implicated). But they did him very well there. He had comfortable quarters and his own servants to look after him. He met some interesting people, too, among them Sir Walter Raleigh, another inmate. He got whatever books he wanted, and, but for the fact that your head might be cut off, it might have been a very good gentlemen's club. He and Raleigh dabbled in literature and chemical experiments. Sir Walter invented an elixir, a formidable quack stimulant: my ancestor and he both throve on it until Raleigh lost his head.

As a bookish man, my ancestor ought to have been happy in the Tower, but he wasn't. Although he wasn't an out-of-doors man, he longed for the freedom to say, for example, 'No, I won't go out hunting today.' So he bought his liberty with a ransom of £11,000, went home, and pursued the same indoor bookish existence as he had in the Tower. I used to think that he might just as well have been back inside instead of having paid that ransom to King James I. But, of course, the thing is to be able to say that you *want* to stay indoors, not that you have *got* to stay indoors.

The £11,000 – a hefty sum in those days – seems to have thwarted his plans for the rebuilding of Petworth, where he spent his remaining years in scientific and alchemical experiments and earned the nickname of 'The Wizard Earl'.

His son Algernon, the 10th Earl, achieved the improbable feat during the Civil War of sitting on the fence with his ears to the ground, thereby remaining on friendly terms with both sides. For a time he was entrusted by the Parliamentarians with the care of the younger children of King Charles I, a duty which he carried out with the greatest kindness. His son Joscelyn survived him by only two years. Joscelyn died in 1670 at the age of twenty-six, leaving an only daughter, Elizabeth, as heiress to the huge Percy estates.

Lady Elizabeth was left in the keeping of her mother until the latter might marry again, whereupon the guardianship was to revert to Elizabeth's grandmother, a Howard, daughter of the 2nd Earl of Suffolk. Well, Lady Elizabeth's mother did marry again only a year later: she married the English Ambassador in Paris, Montague. Whereupon Elizabeth fell into the keeping of her grandmother, a dowager vixen – proud, ruthless and overbearing. Sacrificed to her grandmother's ambition, the unhappy child was given in marriage three times before her sixteenth birthday. Charles II sought her hand for one of his bastards and was turned down.

As husband for Elizabeth, the dreadful dowager selected the half-witted and grotesque but rich Lord Ogle, heir to the Earl of Newcastle. To this awful creature Elizabeth Percy was married in 1679 when still only twelve years of age. He was little older. He died six months later.

In 1681 a dashing adventurer, Count Königsmark, appeared on the scene. He fell in love with the fourteen-year-old widow. But it was all quite blameless. She was then made to marry instead one of the rips of the Duke of Monmouth's set – Thomas Thynne of Longleat. The wedding-night was frightful, and in the small hours of the morning Elizabeth disappeared and was next heard of in the care of an older and kind friend, Lady Temple, with whom she had taken refuge from an all-too-battered rake.

Thynne was subsequently murdered in a brawl, which served him right. His death must have been a great relief to the still very young Lady Elizabeth. But the dreadful grandmother was soon negotiating for a third marriage – this time to the 6th Duke of Somerset. And it came about. (Oddly enough, there was a gentle, kind, charming 3rd Duke of Somerset who had loved Lady Elizabeth's mother, but she had turned him down.)

The 6th Duke of Somerset was one of the most pompous lords ever. He was born a younger son with no great expectations. By a concatenation of circumstances, including the murder of his elder brother Francis by an outraged Italian whose wife Francis had affronted in a church near Genoa, he succeeded to the dukedom, which had descended to Francis from a cousin.

A contemporary duke, the Duke of Marlborough, thought Somerset too witless to be employed 'in anything that is of any consequence'. Fundamentally, however, although pompous and therefore unattractive, Somerset was a decent man and a lot more upright than many of his contemporaries. He was just inordinately proud, and was known as 'The Proud Duke'.

Stupid he may have been, but he always stood up for his principles. When he was First Lord of the Bedchamber to King James II, he was assigned the duty of introducing at St James's the Pope's representative, whom the King was determined to receive publicly and officially. The Duke refused. He said that such a performance would subject him to heavy penalty under the law of the land; whereupon the King insulted the Duke by saying that he would have His Grace fear him as well as the law. The Duke insulted the King back, as well as one could do in those days, by replying that he could not fear the King as long as he committed no offence, because he was sure that he was secure in His Majesty's justice – which, as he knew very well, he wasn't. He lost his place and his regiment, but the people admired his spirited conduct.

The Duke supported the Prince of Orange in 1688. King William thought little of him, however. He and his wife were favourites of Princess Anne. In 1692, when the courtiers were forbidden to countenance the Princess, the bold Somerset had her welcomed at one of his houses, Syon. Anne when she became Queen made him Master of the Horse. Much as he loved ceremony and all the grandeur that went with great offices of state, he didn't allow this to interfere with his conscience. Somerset backed up the Duke of Marlborough in 1708, when, at the instance of Harley, then at the head of the Government, it was proposed to sack Marlborough. Up spoke the proud Duke of Somerset against 'that fellow' (pointing at Harley) for dealing with war policy without the advice of Marlborough. He may have been pompous, but Marlborough was wrong in saying that he was witless, and he helped to save Marlborough's career.

When Queen Anne lay dying, Somerset suddenly appeared at a meeting of the Privy Council, which he had not attended for some years, and, supported by Lord Shrewsbury, Lord Somers and the Duke of Argyll, helped to ensure the succession of George I.

The new King reinstated him as Master of the Horse. Two years later, after being refused permission to bail his son-in-law, Sir William Wyndham, who was suspected of corresponding with the Pretender, he resigned his Mastership and delivered up his insignia and royal livery by having them pitched into a dustcart and ordering his servants to 'shoot all the rubbish' into the courtyard of St James's Palace. This they dutifully did.

The Duke of Somerset was the man who built Petworth House as we know it today. Formerly it had been a manor house. He turned it into a palace. He was able to do this because his wife had brought him a huge fortune, and he lost no time in spending it.

'The Proud Duke' remained proud to the end. But when his first wife, Elizabeth, died, and he was looking for another, his pride took a tumble. His eyes fell on the lady who had now become the widow of his old critic, the Duke of Marlborough. The proud Duke wrote and proposed to the Duchess of Marlborough. But he got his come-uppance from her all right. She wrote back: 'If I were young and handsome as I was instead of old and faded as I am, and you could lay the empire of the world at my feet, you should never share the heart and hand which once belonged to John Duke of Marlborough.'

Undaunted, he married Charlotte, third daughter of Daniel Finch, 2nd Earl of Nottingham. He is said to have remarked when his second Duchess tapped him with her fan: 'Madam, my first Duchess was a Percy, and *she* never took such a liberty.' He would not let his children sit down in his presence. When one of his daughters did so while he was asleep, and he woke up and found her sitting there, he changed his will, leaving her £20,000 the poorer. His servants obeyed him by signs, and, when he travelled, the country roads were scoured by outriders whose duty it was to keep the vulgar out of the way.

Of the old Percy manor house at Petworth not much remains except the thirteenth-century chapel and some seventeenth-century work in the north-east part of the house. Between 1688 and 1696 Petworth was almost wholly rebuilt by 'The Proud Duke', who gave the house its present form and the magnificent elevation on the west front. This façade, 320 feet long, built of local stone, with Portland for the ornamental features, suffers today from the loss of the central dome which once gave vertical emphasis to the composition and was later removed. The Duke of Somerset's exterior shows marked French characteristics and was at one time ascribed to Pierre Puget. But recent researches by Sir Anthony Blunt show that it was more probably built by an English architect, interpreting in his own unorthodox manner French architectural designs that were already out of fashion on the Continent when Petworth was rebuilt. Mr G. H. Kenyon has discovered in the Petworth archives a payment in 1690 to 'Mr. Scarbrow a surveyor for 8 days measuring . . . £10.15.0.' It is therefore probable that John Scarborough, who was frequently employed by Wren and became Clerk of the Works at Greenwich, had a hand in the building of the house.

The exterior of the late seventeenth-century house remained little altered until 1869–72, when the architect Salvin replanned and rebuilt the south front and did it rather well. Less successfully he also arranged a new entrance and porch on the east front. The principal entry had previously been into the Marble Hall from the park on the west.

When 'The Proud Duke' died in 1748 he was succeeded by his son Algernon, who in the following year was granted by George II, among other honours, the earldoms of Northumberland and Egremont. When Algernon died in 1750, however, he left no son, and his estates and titles were divided. Algernon's son-in-law, Sir Hugh Smithson, changed his name to Percy and took the earldom of

Northumberland (subsequently raised to a dukedom) and the estates now held by his descendant, the present Duke of Northumberland. Petworth, Cockermouth in Cumberland and other lands went to Charles Wyndham, the son of Algernon's sister Catherine, who had married Sir William Wyndham. Sir William came of a long line of Norfolk squires, one of whom, in the sixteenth century, had married into a Somerset family and settled at Orchard Wyndham in that county. Sir William, like many of his family from the earliest times, was a Member of Parliament. He was a High Tory and a great friend of Lord Bolingbroke. He served under Queen Anne at an early age as Secretary for War and then Chancellor of the Exchequer.

Sir William was a great gentleman with a certain amount of ability, but not a great statesman. He had a curious experience with fortune-tellers. As we all know, it is a great mistake to tempt Fortune. Napoleon made a mistake about Fortune: he said that Fortune was a woman: he went on to say that the more she did for him the more he would require of her. Look what Fortune did for him in the end! Fortune diddled him.

Well, Sir William Wyndham, on coming down from Oxford, did the Grand Tour. In Venice a fortune-teller told him to beware of a white horse. William didn't think much about it, but soon after his return to England, when out for a walk near Charing Cross, he saw a lot of people going in and out of a house and asked what was happening. He was told that Duncan Campbell, a deaf-and-dumb soothsayer and purveyor of miraculous cures, was doing business there. William went in and was startled to be warned again to beware of a white horse. How Duncan Campbell in his condition communicated with his clients I do not know, but what I do know is that he put the wind up

William, who decided there and then that he had better be careful about the colour of his horses.

In 1715 William was arrested as a Jacobite and taken to the Tower of London. As he was led into the Tower he looked up, and, lo and behold, there was the white horse of the Hanover coat-of-arms over the gateway. So *that* was what they meant, thought William. After his release he took care not to get into trouble again with King George and so regarded the portent as laid. But he was wrong, for later he was thrown from a white horse and kicked. He nevertheless survived. Had he been killed, this story would have been neater. Fortune is untidy. When William eventually died in his bed, Pope wrote : 'If I see any man merry within a week after this death, I will affirm him no true patriot.'

William Wyndham's experience with the fortunetellers reminds me of an incident in the life of another – and earlier – relative of mine, Harry Hotspur. On 21 July 1403, just before the Battle of Shrewsbury, Harry called for his favourite sword. They had to tell him that it had been left behind in a neighbouring village called Berwick, where he had spent the previous night without noticing the name. Harry turned pale and said, 'Then has my plough reached its last furrow.' He had once been warned by a soothsayer that he would die near Berwick. As a Border fighter, he had taken the soothsayer to mean Berwick-on-Tweed. He had never heard of a place called Berwick in Shropshire. Shortly after midday the opposing side put out their banners. Battle was joined, and Harry Hotspur was killed.

Sir William Wyndham's son Charles, who was to inherit the earldom of Egremont, dabbled in love and at one stage got rather deeply involved with what was then considered an unsuitable girl in Paris. The answer to the problem – what to do about Charles – was produced by Lord Bolingbroke, at that time in exile in France.

Charles had become entangled with an actress, Mademoiselle Gossein. Lord Bolingbroke, for the sake of his old friend, Charles's father, was anxious to get Charles out of it. Now there is no one better than a roué to prevent somebody else from becoming one if he is so minded. Bolingbroke's solution was to throw the boy and girl together as much as possible. He wrote to Charles:

I want to know several circumstances about your present passion which I hope and believe scarce rises above your waist. If it be for the Gossein, or the d'Angerville, the two only ladies of the Comédie that I know by sight you must tell me which. I want likewise to know whether you are happy and by what medium, whether by money or stark love and kindness. With ladies, with those particularly, good Ingeniers proceed by assaults, not by saps. If you have enjoyed, stick to her close, work yourself hard, she will like you the more and you will like her the less for it. Whilst I loved much, I never loved long, but was inconstant to all for the sake of all. If you have not enjoyed, make a fair push, triumph or quit. Above all things, let her have no hopes of your sighing, or fears of your being incommoded.

For his part, Charles wrote a youthful poem about his dear love, whom he called the Fair Thief. She had stolen the whiteness of the snow, the blushes of the dawn, the Graces' silken smiles, Juno's dignity, Pallas's sense to charm the soul, Apollo's wit, a Muse's skill and more. Charles concluded:

> Great Jove approved her crimes and art;
> And, t'other day, she stole my heart!
> If lovers, Cupid, are thy care,
> Exert thy vengeance on this Fair:
> To trial bring her stolen charms,
> And let her prison be my arms!

But Bolingbroke's advice worked. Charles ended up by marrying the daughter of an Irish peer, became a Secretary of State, and rather gross.

When in 1763 the famous, gay, clever, ugly, squinting, charming, raffish Opposition politician and publicist, John Wilkes, was arrested for the publication of the forty-fifth number of *The North Briton*, and was interviewed by the Secretaries of State, he looked one of them, Charles, now Lord Egremont, straight in the face and suggested that if he were to be imprisoned in the Tower he might have the same room as had once been occupied by Sir William Wyndham. It was a good jest in trying circumstances; it did not save him from the Tower. But Charles Egremont was the opposite of his High Tory father, Sir William. He was an independent, devoted to no political cause, and a poor speaker, lacking in Parliamentary gifts.

One day in 1763 Charles was heard to say genially, 'Well, I have but three more turtle dinners to come and if I survive them I shall be immortal.' He didn't and wasn't. He died of apoplexy at Egremont House, Piccadilly, now the Naval and Military Club.

He left a large sum invested in the 4 per cent annuities raised for the war in 1761 – 'a loan for glory', rejected by Horace Walpole who said, 'I had rather have a bronze than a thousand pounds in the stocks.' Egremont had both.

Charles, Lord Egremont was succeeded by his son George, a remarkable man born in 1751, who died in 1837. Sir William Beechey, R.A., said of him that 'putupability' was one of his nicest characteristics, meaning the amount that he could bear before taking the trouble to be angry.

This Lord Egremont, the 3rd Earl, was humane, cultured, observant, sprightly, accurate, shrewd, eccentric, benevolent, well grounded in the classics, of literary and artistic bent, highly competent in business and all practical affairs, a leading landowner and agricultural reformer, Lord Lieutenant of his county in the most literal sense of the term, and a winner of five Derbys and five Oaks, all but one with horses bred by himself.

Burke spoke of him as 'delighting to reign in the dispensation of happiness'. This was true. But he was shy, and he preferred the company of artists and agriculturists to that of grandees.

He got engaged to Lady Maria Waldegrave, a stepdaughter of the Duke of Gloucester and a great-granddaughter of Sir Robert Walpole. On 5 July 1780 there was a party at Ranelagh at which the Gloucesters were present to celebrate the event. Egremont being a grandson of the Tory leader, Sir William Wyndham, who had been Walpole's enemy, it was pleasant to reflect that differences instead of being carried on from generation to generation might now be resolved. The company at Ranelagh were all agog. Their whisperings and pointings made Egremont feel so uncomfortable that he broke off the engagement – which shows that there were *some* things with which he would not put up.

He neither drank nor gambled. Wine made him uncomfortable; and he thought that the constant gains of some players weren't due to chance alone. A friend of his, Lord Hertford, took a different line. When asked what he would do if he saw a man cheating at cards, Lord Hertford replied, 'Bet upon him, to be sure.'

That the gains of some players were not due to chance alone is borne out by the diaries of George Egremont's cousin, the first Duchess of Northumberland:

October, 1767 – At the October Meeting at Newmarket, 1767, an odd Event happened. My Lord engaged in a Party at Whist

*Henry Percy, 9th Earl of Northumberland, 'The Wizard Earl'
by Van Dyck*

Charles, 6th Duke of Somerset, known as 'The Proud Duke', and his wife, Elizabeth Percy; both by Kneller

with Mr. M., Mr. R. V. & Mr. B, among the sitters by was
Major Brereton who after some time said he could not be sitting
by & seeing my Lord lose his Money and be so egregiously
impos'd on as he was by the party with whom he play'd & tax'd
them before their Faces with being in a Confederacy to cheat my
Lord and making signs to each other of the number of Trumps he
held in his Hand & described the manner in wch. they made
them by a Stick on wch. they put their Fingers so as to inform
each other of the number. They as may be imagined deny'd it
and he with the utmost Vehemence attested it, & put an End to
the Party, My Lord remaining quite neuter in the Affair.

They could be pretty rough in those days. Major
Brereton was a noted gambler. Sheridan, the politician and
dramatist, met him one day after a long interval. Brereton
said to Sheridan : 'I have had a great misfortune since we
met before : I have lost Mrs Brereton.' 'How did you lose
her ?' asked Sheridan. 'At hazard or at quinze ?'

George Egremont was generous to people in all walks of
life – artisans, artists and duchesses. The painter Turner
was his frequent guest at Petworth. Under him, Petworth
House was like a huge inn with visitors coming and going
as they pleased : they were welcome without notice.
There was no leave-taking either : you didn't say goodbye,
you just left. Guests found themselves confronted with
nurses and babies, girls exercising the pianoforte, boys
exercising ponies. Nobody was ever quite sure whose
children they were. There were artists all over the place,
some doing original works, others copying Vandycks. In
the Old Library you might have discovered Sir William
Beechey altering the figure and background of Gainsborough's portrait of Egremont's mother (what a mistake,
I always think, whenever I look at that portrait as I sit at
my desk in the Red Library, where it now hangs). Then

c

there would be Carew, the sculptor, modelling and messing about in his bedroom, or chiselling a medallion or two downstairs.

The great Turner first arrived at Petworth in 1809. He was given a room to work in, and one of his watercolours in the British Museum shows him working there. He kept the door locked: no one but Egremont was allowed in. Today we have twenty-two Turner pictures at Petworth, and they are among the most precious possessions of the house. The Turner Room, where some of them are hung, is lit up on the dullest of days by these pictures coruscating on lion-coloured walls and reflected in a big rococo looking-glass set between the windows. Light was the ally with which Turner carried all before him, filling his pictures with impalpable and haunting presences.

Turner was a brilliant curmudgeon. When somebody fatuously said to him, of one of his pictures: 'Yes, but, you know, I never see sunsets as you paint them,' Turner retorted: 'No, but wouldn't you like to!'

Eventually he became so mad about painting that he felt that only an artist could understand it – and to hell with everybody else. When a friendly visitor, the Rev. Mr Kingsley, told him that his mother had liked the picture *Snow Storm: Steamboat off a Harbour's Mouth*, Turner snubbed him:

'I did not paint it to be understood, but I wished to show what such a scene was like: I got the sailors to lash me to the mast to observe it; I was lashed for four hours, and I did not expect to escape, but I felt bound to record it if I did. But no one had any business to like the picture.'

'But my mother once went through such a scene, and it brought it all back to her.'

'Is your mother a painter?'

'No.'

'Then she ought to have been thinking of something else.'

Yet, surprisingly enough, Turner often said that if he could have begun life again he would rather have been an architect. He was the miserly son of a miserly London barber: 'Dad never praised me except for saving a shilling.' But, outside painting, preoccupation with concupiscence exceeded even his passion for money. Turner and Carew, the sculptor, were once fishing in the lake at Petworth, when Carew, in his blunt Irish way, broke silence and said:

'Turner, they tell me you're very rich.'

'Am I?'

'Yes; everybody says so.'

'Ah! I would give it all up to be twenty years of age again.'

'What! Do you like it as well as all that?'

'Yes, I do.'

When he had it he wasn't too particular, either. There are legends about sordid carryings-on in squalid brothels and taverns in Wapping.

After his death, Ruskin, going through the sketches and drawings which were part of Turner's treasury to the nation, was startled to find some very erotic stuff. W. M. Rossetti, who had been helping Ruskin to sort the things out, thought them 'from the nature of their subjects undesirable to preserve'. So Ruskin burned them on the authority of the Trustees of the National Gallery. Turner's private life was his own business; and about it, the Trustees of the National Gallery considered, the rest of us should mind ours.

As to Turner and money, his contemporary, the engraver Lupton, says:

When asked the price of a picture by a purchaser he would say two hundred guineas. The reply has been, 'No, I will give you one hundred & seventy five.' 'No, I won't take it.' On the morrow the applicant for the picture has come again. 'Well, Mr. Turner, I suppose I must give you your price for that picture : the two hundred guineas.' Mr. Turner has been known to reply : 'Ah, that was my price yesterday, but I have changed my mind also; the price of the picture today is two hundred and twenty five guineas.' The applicant went away, and perhaps the next day was glad to have the picture at another increased price.

Well, that was Turner's own business too.

But in a more understanding and, I trust, a more compassionate age many would prefer to know as much as possible about a great man in order to understand the whole. I could wish that Ruskin hadn't burned those sketches.

One night in 1834, when Turner, with his fellow artists Constable, Phillips and Leslie and Leslie's family were staying at Petworth, their host put on a fireworks display in the park. As the rockets soared into the sky Leslie's little girl squeaked up and said : 'Won't God be shot?' This pleased Constable's personal belief in the artistic supremacy of skies. It is not recorded that Turner said anything. But what he might have said was that God was out of sight just now, because, as he said when he was dying, 'The sun is God.'

As to duchesses, here is a letter from the beautiful and extravagant Georgiana Duchess of Devonshire :

My Dearest Lord Egremont,

I write from Chiswick where I am very desirous to stay but alas unless you can for this once exert yourself for me I must return to town tonight. If you have the goodness to post me a draft for £300 for tomorrow in a blank cover. . . .

She promised to repay it next Saturday. A draft for £300 was sent, and the next letter from the Duchess asks for a postponement.

This Lord Egremont became quite bored with the *haut monde* and retired to Petworth, preferring to hobnob with artists like Turner and agriculturists like Arthur Young – and with a Miss Iliffe who bore him six bastards before he eventually married her. On 16 July 1801 she became his lawful wife, but the marriage that should have established her position destroyed it. An adjustment to the changed circumstances proved too difficult for both of them. A deed of separation and settlement was executed in May 1803, and she left Petworth never to return. In the meantime one legitimate daughter was born, only to die in infancy. I have inherited Petworth through the illegitimate line. What happened, I suppose, was that Miss Iliffe, when she came downstairs as a wife after being kept upstairs as a mistress, started bossing the servants about and interfering with Egremont's arrangements and disturbing his comfort. He needed a mistress but he could not manage a wife.

As to the girl who was born in wedlock, I remember once dining alone at Petworth with my Uncle Charles Leconfield, my predecessor there, and discussing family affairs. I mentioned the legitimate girl and said : 'It was a good thing she wasn't born a son and survived, wasn't it, Uncle Charles ?'

'My dear boy, it doesn't bear thinking of!'

Nevertheless the 'putupability' remained. When the *haut monde* continued to arrive, George put up with them and put them up. He would wander through the great rooms, his hat on his head, his hands in his pockets and little dogs at his heels, exchanging civilities whenever he felt obliged to do so.

That his eldest son, who was to inherit his estates, would not also inherit his titles caused him neither embarrassment nor regret. He repeatedly refused the Garter. He expressed the keenest pleasure when Lord Melbourne (whose mother had been a great and good friend of his) 'declined being made a monkey of by having a blue ribbon tied round his neck and his nickname changed from Viscount to Earl'. His contempt for such things he attributed to 'something wrong in my natural construction'.

What was wrong in Egremont's natural construction I am not qualified to say. For all his benevolence and for all the happiness that he dispensed, I doubt whether he was happy himself. For such happiness as we may aspire to on this earth a more direct nature is required – for example that of a more recent paladin who, having accepted the Garter, was asked what the installation ceremony at Windsor was like and replied : 'My dear fellow, it was marvellous : it was, don't you know, like a mixture between Holy Communion and getting your house colours.'

An aunt of mine once said to me that what she chiefly enjoyed were expeditions. She meant family outings. I don't like them. *Inpeditions*, if I may coin a word, are what I really like – browsing about at home. Mr Wilde once said that he would rather talk than walk. I am thriving when not driving. Not so most of my relatives.

Starting on 12 September 1805, George, Lord Egremont went on an expedition. He arranged it through a man called Socket, who was tutor to his sons and also his general factotum.

The party consisted of Egremont, Miss Fanny Wyndham, his eldest daughter, two younger daughters with Mademoiselle Lord, who was their French governess, Socket, and a servant, Carleton. Fanny didn't want to go, but she went, and she was a wet blanket. Socket refers to Fanny in his diary as 'Miss W.'

Socket writes :

1805 – Septr 12 (Thursday Went to Chichester with L^d E and all the family – from C we went on to Stanstead (late the residence & property of Mr. Barwell but since his death purchased by a Mr. Way) – They would not let us see the inside of the house.

Stanstead is now the residence of Lord Bessborough.

Then they went on to Portsmouth :

we put up at the George but could not get any beds in the house which was very full owing partly to the arrival of people from India & partly to there being several people belonging to Ld Nelson who was hourly expected.

13 Friday – L^d E hired a sailing boat & we set off for Spithead with an intention of going on board the Victory but when we came near her they were getting under way for St. Helens and of course we could not go on board however we lay to and saw her anchors got up and accompanied her part of the way to St. Helens when we hauled our wind and made for Ride which as the wind was directly contrary we did not reach without 2 or 3 tacks. After taking some refreshment at Ride we set off to walk towards St. Helens we saw the house and grounds of a Mr. Simeon . . . We then went on to *the Priory* the Seat of Judge Grose from whose grounds the view is very beautiful but not to be compared I think to that from Mr. Simeon's . . . the Judge however has the pleasure of completely commanding the Road of St. Helens & we could now see very distinctly the Victory which had brought up there & was (as it was said) only waiting Ld Nelson arrival on board to put to Sea.

At about 7 p.m. they got back on board the sailing boat to return to Portsmouth. By this time Fanny was bored with the expedition and started to play up. No sooner had the boat sailed than she said that she felt qualmy. This set off Mademoiselle Lord and the two younger girls, who were sick. A bad time was had by all, and Fanny was getting on Socket's nerves. But there was worse to come :

When we got there Miss W could eat no dinner because she had been told in the morning that an Officer just arrived from India was lying dead in the house and she fancied that all the people of the Inn would be touching him and then handling the victuals – I was sorry to see that a young lady so very amiable as she should give way to so absurd a weakness – how is she ever to get thro the world? surely tho mildness & gentleness of manners is a great recommendation to any person yet a certain degree of firmness is not less so – when mildness and gentleness are carried beyond a certain point they degenerate into real weaknesses.

Then Socket sees Lord Nelson:

Saturday 14 Carleton informed me this morning when he came to call us (about 7) that Lord Nelson had been arrived above an hour – I got up & dressed myself immediately & went to the Inn where I found so great a crowd in the gateway that it was not without some exertion that I could gain admittance – just as I got to the foot of the stairs I met Ld Nelson full dressed with 3 or 4 stars on his breast he seemed very anxious to get on board – soon after L^d N went out into the street to call on somebody when he was followed by a number of people who crowded after him in all directions eager to the greatest degree to gain a sight of him. I was amused by the eagerness of a common sailor I met who was running with all his might and who, on being asked by another if he had seen *him* replied no but D——n the old B——r I *should* like to see him once more – & away he posted full speed – this I suppose to be the utmost expression of nautical affection – L^d N left Portsmouth about one to go on board the Victory & it is said he is to sail immediately.

So Lord Nelson did – and the end was Trafalgar.

The next year Egremont offered Socket the opportunity of becoming the Rector of Petworth. The only trouble was that Socket was not a clergyman. Well then, make him one. Socket writes in his diary :

Towards the end of June Lord E one day after dinner we being alone proposed to me to go into orders & at the same time in the kindest and most liberal manner offered to give me the living of Petworth – I was much gratified by the proposal in every point of view – the offer of liberal & independent establishment is pleasing but infinitely more so to my feelings is the idea that my conduct has been such as to give satisfaction than which I think there cannot be a more convincing proof that L^d E's wishing to settle me close to his own door – were he not satisfied with my past conduct & confident of my future good behaviour he would find some other mode of remuneration.

Having the idea of going into the Church I thought it would be advisable to enter at one of the Universities & to take a degree or not as might afterwards best suit my convenience accordingly on the 12 of July when L^d E & the family left town for Petworth I went to Oxford.

He was speedily matriculated.

Egremont now started badgering the Bishop of Chichester, because he wanted Socket back to tutor his youngest son, Charles.

Socket writes in his diary :

1807 March 8 (Oxford) L^d E waited on the B^p at Chichester ab^t the beginning of Septr and asked him to ordain me which he refused saying that he could not do it unless I had taken a degree in consequence of which refusal L^d E determined that I should keep my terms at Oxford as fast as possible & permitted me to take Charles with me – I arrived at Oxford on the 14th Oct^r & left it the 11th Nov^r – We went thro' to Petworth in one day & staid there till Feby 16 when we return to Oxford.

I cannot in this part of my Journal omit mentioning tho I know not how to express my feelings as I would wish of the kindness L^d E has shewn towards me with respect to my keeping terms at Oxford – he permits me to have Charles with me, & a Servant & bears every expense in the most delicate & liberal manner.

He *is* a Patron.

And there, appropriately enough, the diary ends. Socket got his degree – and the living.

George Egremont became such a popular figure in his home county that his birthday became a great festival, with ringing of church bells and a feast for the women and children. In 1834 he was ill at the time of his birthday in December, and so the feast to celebrate it was postponed until he had recovered in May. Greville the diarist attended the feast and has left an account :

a fine sight it was; fifty-four tables, each fifty feet long, were placed in a vast semicircle on the lawn before the house. Nothing could be more amusing than to look at the preparations. The tables were all spread with cloths, and plates, and dishes; two great tents were erected in the middle to receive the provisions, which were conveyed in carts, like ammunition. Plum puddings and loaves were piled like canon-balls, and innumerable joints of boiled and roast beef were spread out, while hot joints were prepared in the kitchen, and sent forth as soon as the firing of guns announced the hour of the feast. Tickets were given to the inhabitants of a certain district, and the number was about 4000; but, as many more came, the Old Peer could not endure that there should be anybody hungering outside the gates, and he went out himself and ordered the barriers to be taken down and admittance given to all. They think 6000 were fed. Gentlemen from the neighbourhood carved for them, and waiters were provided from among the peasantry. . . . A band of musick paraded round, playing gay airs. The day was glorious – an unclouded sky and soft southern breeze. Nothing could exceed the pleasure of that fine old fellow; he was in and out of the windows of his room twenty times, enjoying the sight of these poor wretches, all attired in their best, cramming themselves and their brats with as much as they could devour, and snatching a day of relaxation and happiness.

Then followed fireworks; and before the day ended ten thousand people are said to have assembled. One thousand yards of table-cloth were bought for the occasion. The dinner consisted of eleven hundred stone of meat, a thousand plum puddings, bread, potatoes, salad, and abundance of beer. Two hundred dozen mugs came from London, and the rest were collected locally.

There is a family belief, though I have not been able to substantiate it, that George Egremont's death was hastened by the sad discovery that he had been systematic-ally robbed by his servants, to whom he had always been kind. People in large houses were often robbed by their servants in those days. They had plenty of money and no auditors. Most of them seem to have put up with it – far less trouble than to complain, I suppose. It wasn't just in England, of course. Alexandre Dumas *père*, a most kind-hearted and generous man, had been away from Paris on one of his many trips abroad, and with his usual muni-ficence had allowed his friends the run of his house and cellar during his absence. On his return he gave a great breakfast to celebrate the event. His numerous guests, towards the end of the repast, expressed a wish to drink his health in champagne. He sent a servant downstairs to get some. The servant came back and said that there was none left. Dumas slipped a few Napoleons into the man's hand and told him to run round the corner and buy some. But then, becoming suspicious, he followed the servant, to find him emerging from his own cellar with his own champagne.

The servant begged Dumas's mercy. 'Well, I will forgive you this time', said the writer, '*mais au moins une autre fois faites-moi crédit.*'

One should not be surprised that at a time when everybody was getting richer except the poor, the rich were robbed by their servants.

One of George Egremont's sons, Henry Wyndham, distinguished himself in the Peninsular War. When the French were retreating after the Battle of Vittoria, Henry's was the leading squadron in pursuit. They were following a road blocked by carriages, baggage-wagons, refugees and what not. Henry and his squadron nevertheless pushed on regardless until they caught up with a huge covered carriage with a cavalry escort belonging to the enemy. Forcing his way through the refugees, Henry rode up to the carriage and discharged his pistol through the nearside window. The carriage stopped. The offside door flew open and out bounded Joseph Bonaparte, who hurriedly climbed on to a spare horse and escaped. Thus ended King Joseph's reign in Spain.

There is no doubt that Henry was a very gallant officer. At the Battle of Waterloo he fought in the Coldstream Guards. The battle began with a French attack on the château of Hougoumont with the object of tempting the Duke of Wellington to divert troops from his centre and so weaken the opposition to Napoleon's main attack, which was to be made against the British centre by D'Erlon's infantry. Wellington diverted no troops at all. Henry was at Hougoumont. The Guards held out, despite the bringing up of French reserves who drove the Coldstream and 3rd Guards back to the house and its courtyard. The gate was hastily barricaded by its defenders. Then a French subaltern, Legros, wielding an enormous axe, broke through the barrier with some of his men. But Colonel Macdonnell, who was in command, Captain Wyndham, Ensigns Gooch and Harvey, and Sergeant Graham, by sheer force of strength closed the gate, thus trapping Legros and the few of his men who had got through. Then the Frenchmen, fighting bravely, were slain.

A cousin, Charles Wyndham, was in the great cavalry charge which later that day broke up the attack of D'Erlon's infantry columns. My grandmother, when afflicted by a draught at home, used to say that no Wyndham had closed a door since Hougoumont.

One of the objects taken out of King Joseph's carriage was a magnificent silver chamber-pot, now among the proud possessions of the 14th/20th King's Hussars, whose officers once kindly asked me to dine with them. After dinner, the famous pot was produced loaded with champagne, and I was invited to drink. It was a splendid evening with a splendid regiment. The regimental band played throughout, and I got home very late.

Next day, in London, I ran into Prince Dmitri of Russia at luncheon-time. Naturally enough, I was having a light lunch. I explained to the Prince that I had business to do in the afternoon and was trying to get a potful of champagne out of my system. I told him the story of King Joseph's pot. How ridiculous, I said, to have a grand silver chamber-pot in one's carriage. Not at all, said the Prince, 'We all had one.' It was a very sensible thing to have : 'Didn't your family have one, too ?' The Prince then explained that when travelling for considerable distances in a carriage on bad roads a metal utensil was advisable : a china one could get broken. And if you had to have a metal utensil, as indeed you did, then silver was the stuff of which a gentleman had his utensil made.

The Prince said that he could remember travelling as a child in Russia with his English nurse – and a silver pot. Unfortunately, the nurse was rather incompetent about it all. Of course, it would never have done for little Romanovs to be seen relieving themselves in public. Nor could you waste time on the journey – so you did it while the carriage was going full pelt. The trouble was that the English nurse never managed to gauge which way the wind was blowing when she flung the contents out of the window – with the result that the little Prince might arrive at the Winter Palace literally in a mess.

After my conversation with the Prince, I had some researches made in my archives, and the following entry was found in the account roll for the audit period ending Lady Day 1695 :

To Mr. Rogers for 4 silver chamber potts weighing 91 oz. 2 at 5s. 9d. the ounce 25.17.6 for engraving them 0-10-0.

My goodness, so *we* had *four*!

CHAPTER TWO

Later Leconfields

EGREMONT'S eldest (and illegitimate) son George, who succeeded to most of his estates, was created Baron Leconfield by a beneficent Crown as some sort of consolation. He was my great-grandfather and a great huntsman. The famous Nimrod, Charles James Apperley, on visiting Sussex in January 1824 wrote: 'I have reason to believe that the county of Sussex produces the only instance in the sporting world of two brothers each keeping a pack of foxhounds, but so it is.' George was one of them and Henry (the man who captured the chamber-pot) was the other.

There had been hounds at Petworth since the days of the proud Duke of Somerset, who had hunted in the reign of William III.

Around 1800, however, Lord Egremont had reduced his hunting establishment and given his best hounds to the Duke of Richmond. It happened this way. Egremont told his huntsman to take his hounds to the Duke of Richmond's house at Goodwood so that the Duke could pick out whatever hounds he fancied. The Duke on meeting the huntsman said that he was sure that the huntsman knew better than he which were the best hounds, and therefore desired the huntsman to pick them out himself. The Duke

then retired from the scene and the huntsman did the
picking out. When the huntsman was riding home with
his whipper-in and the remaining hounds, he was met at
the lodge gates of Goodwood by the Duke, who instructed
him to take back to the Goodwood kennels the hounds
that he still had with him and swop them for the ones
which he had previously left behind. Thus the Duke got
the best hounds.

The Petworth hounds were in the doldrums until 1817,
by which time the Goodwood hounds, as a result of an
outbreak of rabies in their kennels, had been destroyed.
Then Lord Egremont established a pack for his son
George, who was living at Drove, near Chichester, and a
very good pack it was. Nimrod, when he hunted with
George in 1824, was quite taken with his quiet manner –
'and his hounds were particularly steady and drew as if
they meant to find. . . . I thought Colonel Wyndham rode
very well with his hounds, and his cheering halloo to them
in chase would make an old man's heart feel glad.' The
meet was at New Timber House, six miles from Brighton.
There was a field of about two hundred horsemen.

Egremont's younger son, Henry, was equally keen on
hunting. So while George was hunting from south of
Petworth to the sea, there was room for another pack of
hounds north of Petworth in the Weald, and Egremont
established one for Henry, who was living at Sladeland.

When Egremont died in 1837 he left Petworth and all
his Sussex property (and much more) to George.
George now moved to Petworth and brought his hounds
with him and proceeded to hunt the country which had
previously been hunted by Henry. Henry, as if nothing
had happened, went on hunting it too.

So there were two separate packs of foxhounds with

Sir William Wyndham with his first wife, Lady Catherine Seymour, and two of their children. Charles, in the centre, became the 2nd Earl of Egremont. The painting is by Kneller.

George, 3rd Earl of Egremont, with some of his art collection in the background, by Thomas Phillips

*Petworth House from the lake: dewy morning. Painted by
Turner in 1810.*

*Water colour by Turner of himself painting during one of his
visits to Petworth*

two separate masters hunting the same country at the same time. The result was a dispute which had the local gentry by the ears, gave much copy to the sporting and local press, and permanently estranged the two brothers.

George thought that as he now owned his father's country round Petworth he had the right to hunt it himself. Henry contended that as his hounds had been there first, and as their father had made no stipulation about anybody else having hunting rights, he and his hounds should not be displaced. The fact that George now owned the land was irrelevant. According to hunting law, Henry was probably right. But all the power was George's. George owned the coverts and could forbid them to Henry.

George was shy, taciturn, and solitary – traits which he had inherited from his father without his father's sensibility. Perhaps their bastardy had given him and Henry chips on their shoulders. Anyway they both had vile tempers. Neither brother was an intelligent or cultivated man. George's affections were strong though not diffuse : they embraced his wife, his children and the chase. His wife, a Miss Blunt, was the daughter of an old Sussex family. Wilfrid Scawen Blunt of Crabbet, diarist, poet, revolutionary and breeder of Arabian horses, was her nephew. She was of a very strong evangelical turn of mind.

Henry, after his feats in the Peninsular War and at Waterloo, had become a Lieutenant-General. He had married a daughter of Lord Charles Somerset, but it was a case of holy deadlock. He found consolation in the company of his mistress, a Mrs de la Beche, and deserted his wife.

Relations between George and Henry had not been good for some time. When Henry left his wife the rest of the family adopted an attitude which he greatly resented.

D

Another grievance had to do with the General Election of 1837, in which Henry had not been chosen to represent West Sussex. Henry harboured the suspicion that his candidature had been prejudiced by machinations on the part of the Rev. T. Socket, for many years the friend and factotum of Egremont, and subsequently of George.

When George started hunting at Petworth in 1838 he informed a follower of Henry's hounds, a Mr Napper of Malham, that he did not wish to take his hounds east of Petworth Park. But George soon grew tired of this self-imposed restriction and began hunting to the east without a word to Henry. Finally, on Saturday, 12 December 1838, the two packs clashed. George, who was in London, had directed his huntsman to take his hounds to Flexham Park, a large covert to the east of Petworth, where they had been three times already that season and where they now found Henry with his.

The following Tuesday Mr Napper, on behalf of the gentlemen who hunted with Henry, waited on George at Petworth and remonstrated with him. Napper warned George that if there were recurrences something unpleasant might happen. George lost his temper and Napper went home with a flea in his ear. After he had simmered down, George wrote to Henry expressing his willingness to accommodate him in every way in his power – but he would not allow the interference of a third person.

Henry, in reply, instead of sticking to the point, which concerned nothing but hunting, rehearsed all his old grievances. The conduct of the rest of the family towards him had been 'barbarous'; over the dead body of his father he had hoped for a growth of feeling which might have brought about a reunion of affections and interest; but no; Socket had been brought in, which he regarded

as 'a personal affront to myself'; his (Henry's) offers of
assistance in the winding up of Lord Egremont's affairs
had met with 'cold disdain'; and so on for nearly 700
words, after which he said that although there could be no
difficulty 'on a point so comparatively trifling as hunting',
he could not but feel that George's servants had been sent
to Flexham Park purposely to insult him. The letter
ended:

Trusting the above may be received by you in the spirit that I
conceive it, and leaving every arrangement for the accommodation of hunting to your own convenience and proposal, I beg to
assure you that nothing would give me greater happiness than to
address you as your affectionate brother, H. Wyndham.

There followed an exchange of letters, cool but con-
ciliatory on George's side, heated and offensive on Henry's.
Henry's next one ended: 'Although I have felt that the
mode of acting towards me has been of the most repulsive
and ungenerous kind, yet I still wish to subscribe myself
your affectionate brother, H. Wyndham.' To which
George replied: 'Your hints and your insinuations are
unworthy of you and insulting to me; therefore our
intercourse ceases. G. Wyndham.'

Henry's next effort misfired. He wrote George another
letter – it has not descended to us, but judging from
previous form it was probably a snorter – and, fearing
with good reason that George, if he recognised the writing
on the envelope, would return the letter unopened, got
somebody else to address it. George received the letter
when sitting with a guest, Colonel Kenah. He opened the
envelope and recognised Henry's writing inside. After
getting Colonel Kenah to witness that he had not read it,
he returned the letter to Henry: 'Not knowing the writing
on the envelope, I broke the seal; but I have not read a

syllable of the letter which I return to you. G. Wyndham.'

George now altered his days of hunting for the rest of the season, making them different from those fixed for Henry's hounds. There were no more clashes until the last day of the season, when Henry and his hounds ran into George's west of Petworth Park. Henry probably contrived it deliberately. George thereupon determined to oust Henry and his hounds for good. To this end he drew up an *ex parte* statement which he submitted to three peers who were Masters of Foxhounds. They all agreed that the country should be his. He also got the Duke of Richmond on his side. Fortified by written opinions in his favour from these noblemen, George sent the papers to a Mr King of Loxwood, a gentleman of tact and discretion, who showed them to various others who had been hunting with Henry's hounds.

At this, Henry got out a counter-statement of his own to which Mr King gave equal circulation. Henry excoriated George's statement as an 'attempt to enlist the feelings of large proprietors by stating that the rights of the owner of Petworth are in jeopardy by General Wyndham hunting the country', which (wrote Henry) 'is not only unfair, but absurd.'

For the rest of the year, as you can imagine, the hunting dispute was a great topic of conversation and debate in country houses throughout West Sussex. Both brothers busily canvassed potential supporters. There must have been a lot of heart-searching among the local hunting gentry. Nobody could be sure which brother was going to win, and if they backed the loser they would hardly be welcome followers of the winner's hounds. Some, like Mr Mitford of Tillington and Mr Barttelot of Stopham, backed George. Others, like Mr Napper of Malham, backed Henry. Others

still, like Mr King of Loxwood and Lord Winterton of
Shillinglee, remained neutral. The wily Winterton wrote
to George in May that 'there appears to me to be so much
of family difference intermixed with the subject, that I
cannot think of allowing myself to be drawn into the
contention. At the same time I beg to express my earnest
hope, and what I know to be the desire of all the gentlemen
of our part of the country, that this question may be
amicably settled.' For the rest of the summer his Lordship
confined his sporting interests to cricket.

At least one gentleman, a sporting 'squarson', the Rev.
John Hurst of Thakenham near Storrington, tried to
court both brothers – fatal error! In January 1839 Mr
Hurst wrote to George that he disapproved of Henry's
'whole line of march'. In May he told Henry that he
thought George's attitude 'monstrous'. In June he was
Henry's guest at the latter's London house in Mount
Street, and at Epsom was seen daily in the rumble-seat of
Henry's britzka. In July he told George that he would no
longer preserve foxes for Henry, and he also expressed
the opinion that Mrs de la Beche was responsible for the
insinuations which had ruptured the relations between the
two brothers.

Meanwhile, as a result of the arguments which Henry
and his partisans had been advancing, support had dwindled
for George's contention that, being now the owner of
Petworth, he had the right to displace the hounds already
established and to hunt the country himself. Masters of
Foxhounds who had previously backed George were
changing their minds. Henry argued with great force that
his title to the country was that it had been given to him
unconditionally; and that if George's view was accepted
'the title to every foxhunting country in England would

be shaken.' Small wonder that Masters of Foxhounds changed their minds – though it's a reflection on their intelligence that they had to.

As for George, he changed his tack. Mr King had visited him at Petworth with a bulky bundle of correspondence, all of it unfavourable to George's claim. George refused to read it. His new line was that after Henry's insinuations about his conduct, not only in the hunting field but outside it too, he could not in any circumstances countenance Henry's drawing his coverts.

There was now open warfare between the two brothers. They resorted to pamphleteering. Every bit of material which had any bearing on either the hunting dispute or their private differences was published by one brother or the other. It showed, among other things, that the Rev. T. Socket's conduct in the 1837 election had been all right, and it included a letter to Henry in which George had written about Mrs de la Beche and the family's attitude to her: 'In justice to myself, I must declare that although I have taken that decided line which, as a husband and a father, I feel to be right, I have never, either directly or indirectly, tried or wished to influence any other individual in reference to your peculiar position.' It also showed up the Rev. John Hurst, who was roundly denounced on all sides, the *Sporting Review* declaring that his activities were like 'the Iago workings of Iscariot priests'. In a letter to the *Brighton Guardian*, the leading local newspaper, 'A Layman of the Church of England' pilloried Hurst and referred by way of comparison to 'the striking and consolatory instance of the virtue and consistency of the Rev. T. Socket'. To which the editor appended an acid note: 'If "A Layman" knew the internal history of Petworth House during the occupation of its late owner, he would have been silent upon "the *virtue* and *consistency* of the Rev. T. Socket".'

Mrs de la Beche herself entered the fray with feminine dash and emphasis in a letter to the long-suffering Mr King of Loxwood:

Sladeland, 9th July 1839

General Wyndham has shown me, my dear Mr. King, the letter you enclosed him *this morning* from Mr. Hurst to Col. Wyndham. The *whole* line of Mr. Hurst's conduct with regard to ALL parties is unworthy of a clergyman and despicable and contemptible as a man.

It is not the least of his craft and hypocrisy *throwing upon a woman* the odium he has, AND WHICH HE WELL KNOWS TO BE DECIDEDLY FALSE; but no doubt he must think it will eventually answer some purpose of his own *to act as he has done*.

Whatever I have said, I will repeat again, and to Colonel Wyndham himself if he wishes it; and Col. Wyndham has in his own possession, *and has made public* HIMSELF, those sentiments which are expressed in General Wyndham's last letters to Colonel Wyndham.

I cannot conclude this, without, in justice to myself, assuring you that no individual has more deeply or more sincerely LAMENTED the unhappy difference existing between the two brothers than myself, or one who would make any and every personal sacrifice, COULD IT ONLY BE THE MEANS of uniting them, AS I THINK BROTHERS SHOULD BE; and I live in hope the hour *may yet arrive* when Col. Wyndham will COOLLY REFLECT *upon* THE PAST, and that he may yet feel convinced that HE HAS BEEN THE PERSON that has acted too hastily towards a brother that *has ever been*, and I am quite convinced *ever will be*, worthy of his most affectionate and brotherly love.

Believe me,
My dear Mr. King,
Very sincerely yours,
LETITIA de la BECHE

Mr King forwarded this letter to George, who, as was his wont, refused to read it.

George proceeded to act with shameless lack of scruple – but with plenty of courage and resolution. He turned vulpicide. Determined that if he could not usurp the country formerly hunted by Henry, then nobody else should enjoy it either, he ordered the butchery of foxes in all his coverts in that part of Sussex. Thus Henry and his faction were beaten. George won.

Henry retired (with Mrs de la Beche) to Cockermouth Castle in Cumberland, which his father had left to him for life. He represented first Cockermouth and then West Cumberland in the House of Commons. He tried in vain to get his neighbours in Cumberland to receive Mrs de la Beche. They would receive her, they said, when they had news that she had been received at Petworth. Poor Henry! Poor Mrs de la Beche!

Henry lived to a ripe old age. His small library is preserved at Cockermouth Castle. In a number of his books a mysterious excision has been made in the fly-leaves, leaving a rectangular hole. One book, however, must have escaped the notice of the censor, whoever he was, for the fly-leaf is intact, and there, instead of a rectangular hole, is the bold, impulsive signature 'Letitia de la Beche'.

And in the Muniment Room at Petworth there is a dusty, yellow bundle of papers labelled 'Hunting Controversy'.

When George was master of the house they all had to observe very strict conventions at Petworth. Any familiar intercourse with the town was absolutely forbidden: the children and servants were not allowed to go into it. His wife Mary never entered the town except in a carriage. Only once was she ever in a cab in London, when she broke her finger in the door. Thereafter when she went to London the carriage and horses were put on the train with her and she waited at Victoria Station until they were got off and ready to take her to her town house in Grosvenor Place. She would not travel with strangers : the upper servants at Petworth travelled first class and filled the vacant seats in her compartment.

George Leconfield's eldest son was also called Henry, but the favourite son was Percy. Percy and his wife used to spend most of the winter at Petworth, bringing their three children, Mary, George and Guy, a nurse called Horsnaill and a nurserymaid. They were always very welcome, but the accommodation provided for Horsnaill, the nursery-maid and the children was surprising in a house so enor-mous and well-staffed. They occupied two miserable little rooms called the Chapel Rooms, one of which was used as a day nursery; all five slept together in the other. Con-sidering the eighty bedrooms in the house, this seems rather cramped, but possibly it was what the nurse, the nurserymaid and the children preferred, all snug together in their two little rooms in a huge strange house with the wind howling round it on winter nights. The wind at night can make a strange noise as it strikes and soughs round the house – more noise than I have heard in any other house. I don't know why this is so, but it is. Perhaps it is because the wind comes through some gap in the South Downs, and the house is the first important obstacle that it meets.

After their marriage Mary had enjoyed one or two seasons in London – Almack's, the opera, balls and parties. Then she fell under the spell of the strict evangelicalism of Lady Huntingdon and retired almost completely from the world. This may have suited George, but it could have been rough on their daughters, for she suffered great qualms of conscience as to whether it would be right to take them into Society. Happily, common sense prevailed. As an aunt of mine once remarked : 'It is possible to sin in seclusion as well as in Society.' The daughters, Fanny, Blanche and Caroline, were taken to London balls, though it seems that they weren't allowed to waltz.

While their father was quite happy to let them go out in London, he could not stand a lot of strangers at Petworth. So a compromise was arranged. For about six weeks in the year young people were asked to stay; for the rest of the year no one was invited except one or two of his old cronies, such as Admiral Rous. How boring it must have been for the children, with nothing to be heard during the long family dinners except the sound of mastication and talk of the day's run with the hounds, which Fanny, Blanche and Caroline had not experienced as they didn't hunt.

Blanche eventually married Lord Mayo, and my wife is their great-granddaughter. Mayo became Viceroy of India, and a good one. As such he took an interest in the convict settlement on the Andaman Islands. The convicts were put to useful work, like rug-making. A good many of their rugs used to arrive at Petworth with the Viceroy's compliments. It was all in a good cause until the day when Lord Mayo and Blanche paid a visit to the Andaman Islands in their yacht. Mayo was rowed ashore to inspect the settlement, Blanche remaining on board. When he was due to return to the yacht, she went to the side to watch the boat coming back. There it was, sure enough, but she could not distinguish the figure of her husband, whom she expected to see sitting in the stern. She discovered the reason when the boat came alongside and the dead Viceroy was carried out with a knife in his back, implanted by one of the convicts. So there were no more rugs from India at Petworth.

Blanche and the murdered Viceroy had a daughter who married an Irish cousin of mine, Windham Wyndham-Quin, 5th Lord Dunraven. I don't know why my cousins christened their children by the first half of their surnames and then spelt them differently, but they did. This Dunraven's predecessor, the 4th Lord Dunraven, was interested in spiritualism. He therefore sought out D. D. Home, one of the best-known spiritualists of the day. One day, in Dunraven's house, Home said that he felt in the mood for a bit of levitation. He thereupon lay flat on his back and became levitated, floating horizontally about the room. But it was a hot day, and they were upstairs with all the windows wide open. Home floated out through one of the windows.

Dunraven was beside himself with worry. Where was Home going to come down? What if he *crashed*? Dunraven rushed to the window and looked out. He found that Home had turned to port and was now floating slowly alongside the façade of the house. With great presence of mind, Dunraven rushed into the passage and the next-door room and dragged Home through the window by his legs.

This is the sort of scrape that we Wyndhams and Wyndham-Quins are apt to get into. But Dunraven and Home should have known that you must *never* try levitation with the windows open.

After George's wife died in 1863 he never again asked a stranger into Petworth House. Besides Fanny, Blanche and Caroline, there was another daughter, Helen, who was mentally deficient. George lived on in a loneliness shared with Helen, who would dither about doing nothing much except needlework and going for walks in the park in front of the house. Her chief, and perhaps only, diversion was going to tea at the rectory, a few yards' walk from one of the lodges. Her father showed her great kindness and affection, and she seemed devoted to him. When he died, they were all very worried about how to break it to her. Fearing that to a mind already feeble such sad news might be especially damaging, they took care to prepare her as best they could for the blow. She heard them with composure and, when they had finished, she said calmly and with a quiet smile, 'Now at last I can use the down-stairs lavatory.'

George Leconfield was succeeded by my grandfather, Henry, who was

> Handsome and grand
> And idolised land.

He possessed about 110,000 acres. He was addicted, of all things, to complaining about not being an earl. *His* grandfather, who had been one, having delayed getting married to the mother of his children until after six of them were born, the eldest being my great-grandfather, had washed the earldom out for us. A beneficent sovereign, as I have explained, had conferred the barony of Leconfield on my great-grandfather. My grandfather, however, while grateful for this recognition of the family's worth and happy to have inherited the new title, continued neverthe-less to resent that dilatoriness in going to the altar which had done him out of an earldom.

It was my grandfather's King Charles's head. He would go on about it: my aunt Maggie, for example, instead of being a mere Hon. Maggie, might have been the glittering

Lady Margaret. And so on. He would shout about it after dinner, and Maggie (a silly girl) would cry.

Then one morning early in 1886 a letter arrived from the Prime Minister:

My Dear Lord Leconfield,

I have great pleasure in being able to inform you that the Queen has been pleased to confer on you the rank of an Earl – in recognition of your great position and high character. . . .

Believe me,
Yours sincerely,

SALISBURY

Was my grandfather elated? *Au contraire*. Here was his King Charles's head going for a Burton. At first he did not know what to do about it. He brooded over the letter all morning. After mature consideration and a good luncheon, he made up his mind :

Dear Lord Salisbury,

I must beg you to convey to Her Majesty my very grateful acknowledgements for the honour She is so graciously willing to confer on me, but at the same time I trust that Her Majesty will not consider me wanting in appreciation of, and gratitude for her intentions towards me if I decline the rank offered . . .

LECONFIELD

But he was never quite the same after that.

One evening, about the time when bananas were first being imported in any quantity into Britain, my grandfather was dining in the Square Room at Petworth with a friend. The dessert included bananas, and my grandfather, eating one, remarked that he was very fond of them. His guest observed that nobody really knew how good a banana could be unless he had tasted one straight off the tree. My grandfather said nothing at the time, but he minded. He was not going to stand for this sort of Victorian one-upmanship.

Next morning he sent for his head gardener. 'Go', he bade him tersely, 'to Kew. Find out there how to grow a banana. Come back here and grow one.' Off went the head gardener. A special greenhouse was then constructed which might have been the envy of Sir Joseph Paxton himself. The banana tree was splendid. My grandfather took a lively interest in its progress until, lo and behold, it fructified. 'I will have that banana for dinner tonight,' he said as soon as the banana was ripe. And so he did – amid a deathly hush. All were agog. The head gardener himself, controlling a great department of the estate, was not too proud to be there, concealed behind a screen between the dining-room and the serving-room. Even the groom of the chambers broke the habit of a lifetime and turned up sober to watch the event.

The banana was brought in on a lordly dish. My grandfather peeled it with a golden knife. He then cut a sliver off and, with a golden fork, put it in his mouth and carefully tasted it. Whereupon he flung dish, plate, knife, fork and banana on to the floor and shouted, 'Oh God, it tastes just like any other damn banana!' Banana tree and all were ordered to be destroyed. My famous old gardener, Mr Fred Streeter, told me that the banana cost my grandfather some £3,000.

My grandfather was a meticulous man, and to be meticulous is to tempt fate. He had married in 1867, and seventy years later my grandmother, whom we loved, told her grandchildren something about it. On coming up Harting Hill to a beautiful Sussex house, Uppark, where they were to spend their honeymoon, the postilion got off and could not get on again. As my grandmother told us,

'Henry had to go out to assist him and apologised to me afterwards for having said damn in my presence.'

Their first-born, George, was the apple of their eye, and well he might have been. He had charm, good looks and intelligence. Everything was done to encourage George's undoubted ability. The best tutors were engaged to egg him on in the holidays. One of them was an extremely capable young man called Quiller-Couch. Years later, when I was an undergraduate at Cambridge, I met the aged and revered Sir Arthur Quiller-Couch, Professor of English Literature ('Literature,' he would insist, 'is not a mere science to be studied: but an art to be practised'). Q – for it was he who had been George's tutor – was celebrated for his hospitality, his kindness of heart, his humour, his conversation, and the care which he took in choosing and wearing his picturesque clothes. This last-mentioned practice may have been a reaction to be attributed to the time when, very young and poor, he worked long, long hours to support his widowed mother and his two brothers and to pay off some family debts for which he was not responsible.

Anyway, at Cambridge Q spoke to me about George. He told me that George had seemed quite impervious to the exquisite surroundings of his home – yet a line of Virgil could move him nearly to tears, and his first glimpse of Plato affected him much as a child might be dazzled by the light of an unfamiliar doorway half open and surmise the wonderful world within. Q seemed still to be surprised about this. I was not. The grass is always greener on the other side of the fence.

Worse than a *malade imaginaire* is a *médicin imaginaire.* Tragedy can be comic for somebody whom it does not concern : comedy can be tragic for somebody whom it does concern. These thoughts and others occurred to me when on a rainy afternoon I was searching my shelves for a particular book. For me shelves of books are all too often like shoals of red herrings – and that is what they were on this occasion. Before I could find what I was wanting, I happened upon Mr Michael Astor's charming auto-biographical book, *Tribal Feeling*, which I had much enjoyed reading when it was first published by John Murray in 1963. I abandoned my search and browsed through it.

Obviously Michael Astor's father, Lord Astor, had a deep affection for his children. His concern for them and their health drove him to extraordinary lengths. When in the 1920s Lord Astor travelled to Scotland with his family for the summer holidays, he took with him on the train a *cow* and a cowman from the home farm at Cliveden. The cow was milked at Edinburgh and the little Astors nourished without having to drink strange milk. Then the Astors and the train proceeded further north and the cowman and the cow went back to Cliveden. Whether the cowman and the cow were brought back for the return journey, Michael Astor cannot remember; but I should not be surprised if they were. At all events the object of protecting the Astor children from infection, for that was Lord Astor's obsession, was not frustrated. He was lucky. To be meticulous is to tempt fate. Lord Astor got away with it.

Lord Astor had his cow. My grandfather had barrels of water. Lord Astor was obsessed with thoughts about the risk of drinking strange milk. My grandfather dreaded strange water. Whenever the family were in London (by this time they were at 9 Chesterfield Gardens on the corner of Curzon Street : the site is now occupied by the

Two great huntsmen:
George, 1st Baron
Leconfield, by J. E.
Ferneley; and his
brother, Henry, by
George Clint

Uncle Charles, aloft and in the saddle

hideous Leconfield House), he had barrels of drinking-water sent up from Petworth. He always said that he was not going to risk his children catching typhoid fever from drinking the London water. My father, aunts and uncles have told me how, as children, they could gauge the level of the water in the barrel by the degree of its brackish taste in their glasses at table.

This mad business of carting drinking-water from Petworth to Chesterfield Gardens went on until 13 January 1895, when Uncle George died of typhoid fever contracted at Petworth.

Then there was my uncle Charles, who succeeded my grandfather as Lord Leconfield.

One of my favourite dining-rooms at Petworth is the Square Dining-Room. I like it for the memories of dinners which I enjoyed with Uncle Charles in my early youth. I always used to go there for Christmas.

Uncle Charles, although the kindest of men, was taciturn and gruff. We had to dine in white tie and tails. When a gentleman came to stay with only a dinner jacket, and apologised for not having brought his tail-coat, Uncle Charles would offer what he thought the sage advice: 'You should sack your man.' It never entered his head that some of his guests might not have valets.

After one such incident, involving a penniless younger son who was trying to make a start in the world, the young man came down to breakfast in the Square Dining-Room. On one big sideboard were little spirit-lamps burning under a row of copper hotplates with silver dishes containing eggs cooked in various ways, bacon, sausages, kidneys, mushrooms, kippers, kedgeree. On another sideboard was a row of cold meats of almost every kind. Sitting solitary at the table, dressed for hunting and

E

tucking in, was Uncle Charles. In the course of a sub-
stantial meal he uttered two words to the young man. I'm
sure that he didn't mean to be rude : he was just naturally
taciturn. Anyhow, it was the young man's fault. He broke
the silence to ask, 'What hounds are you going out
hunting with, Lord Leconfield?' To which Uncle Charles
replied : 'My own.' He then went on demolishing a huge
and awful black sausage. He was very fond of black
sausage.

In the winter of 1940, at the worst part of the war, I
went down to Petworth to stay with Uncle Charles. The
dinner was, of course, more austere than usual. Uncle
Charles nevertheless drank a bottle of champagne himself
and pressed me to do likewise. We then had some port,
after which we had some brandy.

Uncle Charles lit a cigar and his moroseness temporarily
evaporated, as it always did after dinner. He suggested
that we might go out hunting next day, and I readily
agreed. So out hunting we went : Uncle Charles, his
huntsman, his whipper-in and me. Uncle Charles's hounds
were put in to draw a covert. Some of them hung about in a
ride. This riled him and he screamed : 'Draw, hounds,
draw; otherwise I shall cut you in half.' An old keeper
who was standing by observed, 'Then Your Lordship will
have two packs of hounds, will you not?' Uncle Charles
paid no attention, but when we rode on he spoke well of
the keeper, part of whose beat was an obscure wood, some
miles from any road, called Goachers Furze. This old boy
had once been to London – only once. He said on his
return that he had not enjoyed the visit. While he was
standing in Parliament Square facing the Palace of
Westminster he had asked a cockney what that building

was. The cockney had replied: 'You silly old fool, that is the Houses of Parliament.' 'Silly fool yourself,' said the old keeper. 'I bet if you came to my part of the world you wouldn't know Goachers Furze.' Uncle Charles went on to tell me that the keeper had once killed three thousand pheasants in a morning. He must be a wonderful shot, I said. No, said Uncle Charles, 'It was when he was working for the Rothschilds in France in 1914, and he wrung their necks and sent them to the hospitals.'

We found a fox and lost it, and while Uncle Charles's huntsman was casting for it we heard a tremendous hullabaloo about two miles away. Uncle Charles abused the huntsman and shouted at him: 'Can't you hear a holler?' and bade him, 'Get going thither.' So we galloped in the direction of the noise, only to find that it had nothing to do with fox-hunting: it was a village football match. The hounds, the huntsman, the whipper-in, Uncle Charles and I all slithered to a stop. The footballers and the bystanders who had been making the noise all stopped too. There was silence, then Uncle Charles, who had turned red in the face, stood up in his stirrups and shouted: 'Haven't you people got anything better to do in wartime than play *football?*'

We then went on hunting.

Once, soon after the war, Uncle Charles invited me to luncheon with him at the Travellers' Club in London. I asked him why we were lunching at the Travellers', for I knew that on his rare visits to London he usually lunched at the Turf Club. He explained that he had come up to London for some official function the night before – 'and they have a very good man upstairs here who knows how to put on one's medals and orders properly.'

'Where the M.F.H. dines, he sleeps,' said Mr Jorrocks, 'and where the M.F.H. sleeps, he breakfasts.' Well, where Uncles Charles slept, he lunched also.

After luncheon we moved to a sitting-room. 'Coffee?' said Uncle Charles. He rang the bell. Nobody came. Another member explained that to save manpower the coffee was already in the room and one helped oneself. We were led to a table on which stood a large urn surrounded by coffee cups. Uncle Charles was shown how the thing worked and was told, 'and then you put three-pence in the saucer here.' He started fumbling in his pockets. He tried them all – trouser pockets, jacket pockets, waistcoat pockets – without success: no small change to be found. He turned away and with an air of Roman resignation said: 'It's no good, I am not used to handling small sums.'

When I got married I brought my wife to Petworth to meet Uncle Charles. Although she and I are cousins, she had never met Uncle Charles or been to Petworth before. Looking out of the White Library on a beautiful summer's day, over Capability Brown's park with its stretch of water the size of the Serpentine in the foreground, she said, no doubt wishing to please as well as being entranced by the view, 'Oh, Cousin Charles, what a beautiful lake!' Thunder-laden silence. Then Uncle Charles spoke! 'My dear young lady, one day your husband will inherit from me not only all this, but also, among other things in Cumberland, half Derwentwater, the whole of Bassen-thwaite Lake and the whole of Wastwater, comprising in all about thirty-five square miles of lake. What you see there is not a lake. It is a *pond.*'

But let us now return (from the White Library via the White and Gold Room, the Beauty Room, and the Marble

Hall) to the Square Dining-Room and imagine ourselves once more at dinner there, in the days of my youth. The golden candelabra are throwing a glittering light on the Paul Storr gold and silver plate, the Monteith bowls, the silver wine-coolers on the side-tables, the rococo pier-glasses – and Uncle Charles himself, at the head of the table, is silently pegging his way through a huge bill of fare. He was a great though morose trencherman.

The dining-room table itself was a challenge to all who believed that functional beauty could not be achieved in the mid-nineteenth century. It is a smashing table : I use it still. It was made by a firm in Chichester. Once, for their annual works outing, the Chichester craftsmen chose to come to Petworth to see and admire their table again. There is the pride of proper craftsmanship for you. Arrangements were made for them to put their feet under their own table, and they were properly entertained.

The centrepiece of the table was a huge blue and white Sèvres bowl with the inscription 'Presented to the Earl of Egremont, Secretary of State for Foreign Affairs, by the Duc de Nivernois, French Ambassador, upon the peace of 1763.' In return, Egremont gave the French duke a thoroughbred horse.

You can imagine how lovely the women looked in this candle-lit room. I would have hugged them all had I dared. In the background were the footmen in their blue Wyndham livery with their silver crested buttons agleam. Over all hovered the butler, like a god but often a bit unsteady. To me he seemed a god until one day I heard Uncle Charles remark that one can keep a cellar or a butler, but one cannot keep both. I believe that Uncle Charles had taken this *obiter dictum* from a contemporary, Lord Wimborne.

Pantry work can be the ruin of the drinking classes. When King George VI asked what had happened to one of his servants, was told that he had been dismissed, and inquired why, he received the splendid reply, 'Fuddled in the Presence, Your Majesty.'

There are three long windows in the Square Room with three carved pelmets. Two are the work of an early nineteenth-century carver called Ritson. The third is the work of Mr Hoad, my grandfather's cabinet-maker. Mr Hoad decided that a mallard should be his main subject. My grandfather obligingly went out and shot one for him to use as a model.

Among the paintings on the walls is a splendid Van Dyck of Lord Strafford with lances and tents and a charger in the background. There are also two exotic pictures by Van Dyck of Sir Robert and Lady Shirley. Sir Robert went from a neighbouring house in Sussex, Wiston, to be a diplomatic agent of the Shah of Persia. He picked up Lady Shirley, a noblewoman of Circassian birth, in Isfahan. Any gentleman might well have envied him his choice and luck. There are other pictures, mostly by Van Dyck – the 9th Lord Northumberland, the 10th Lord Northumberland and his Cecil wife and daughter; and Lord Newport, Lord Goring and a page, at least two of whom helped to make a mess of the Civil War. There is a lovely picture of a French hunting scene by Jacques d'Artois and one by Simon Verelst of Prince Rupert, on which Uncle Charles would comment that the Prince looked in the family way.

In this ambiance various interesting things have happened. The Allied Sovereigns came to call in 1814. There is a picture of them doing so. Later on my grandfather had a fight in this dining-room with my great-uncle Percy over the port and their inheritance. Their wives combined to force them subsequently to make it up. My grandfather went to stay with Uncle Percy at Clouds to ratify it and was bitten in the hall by Percy's dog. He kept my grandmother awake most of the night by worrying whether he was going to get hydrophobia. This incidentally annoyed my great-uncle Archie Rosebery, then Prime Minister, who resented other people in his circle being as neurotic as he was.

Then there was Uncle Reggie. We once had a private fire brigade. My father told me that he and his brothers and sisters used to annoy other children at their dancing classes by boasting '*My* father has a fire engine.' Children are apt to boast. My grandfather's fire engine was of the horse-drawn kind with a huge brass boiler on the back. If you lit a fire in the boiler you could get a big pressure of water running through the hoses. But the fire engine was used in earnest only once, when Uncle Reggie was in his early twenties. A small fire had broken out in some cottages by Petworth Church. Uncle Reggie got the fire engine out, had the brass boiler stoked up as it had never been stoked before, and appeared on the scene in a matter of minutes. Other people already had the fire well in hand, but Uncle Reggie insisted on deploying the hoses all the same. Mr Sutton, the Clerk of the Works, shouted, 'Have a care, Mr Reggie.' But to no avail. Uncle Reggie shouted back, 'What are fire engines for?' Whereupon he directed such a fierce jet on the cottages that the whole lot came down.

Uncle Reggie was a bachelor of dash and charm. He hunted and raced a lot and made various hare-brained expeditions about the world. He was partly a pobble, having lost some toes through frostbite on an expedition in Canada. He kept his papers in an old leather hat-box which he used to take about with him, purposely annoying his elder brother, my uncle Charles, by calling it his estate office. Uncle Charles had three proper estate offices dotted about the country.

After my grandfather died, my grandmother had a house at 12 Stanhope Gate, W.1 and Uncle Reggie stayed with her whenever he was in London. My grandmother used to come down to breakfast at nine o'clock. Uncle Reggie would often arrive in the dining-room for breakfast, not via the front stairs, but via the front door, clad in flannels and carrying a racquet, anxious to convey the impression that he had just been playing tennis at Lord's. In fact, he had been sporting with Amaryllis.

He supported a lady in St John's Wood. He also had a loyal Jeeves. His faithful servant would nip up there betimes in the morning with tennis things and winkle Uncle Reggie out. They would then go – Uncle Reggie *le carquois épuisé* – in a cab to Stanhope Gate in time for breakfast. Uncle Reggie's man would get a weary Uncle Reggie out of the cab and up the steps and through the front door into the hall, where Uncle Reggie with a great effort would pull himself together and then go bounding into the dining-room slapping his leg with a racquet: 'Morning, Mother – spot of early morning exercise – feel absolutely whacked – *quite played out.*'

When the 1914–18 war broke out Uncle Reggie managed to disguise his shortage of toes and was killed in action in the first year. They found in his will that he had left a tidy sum to the lady in St John's Wood. My grandmother evinced no surprise. She said nothing about it to anybody, and nobody said anything about it to her, until years later I ventured out of the blue to ask her. She told me that she had soon rumbled Uncle Reggie's St John's

Wood set-up. Reggie and his faithful servant had never deluded her. But their pretence, as she saw it, had been practised out of consideration for *her*. The least that she could do was to pretend to know nothing about it – thus showing equal consideration for *them*.

My grandmother was a wonderful and good woman. She was like a chapel in an eighteenth-century palace, un-profaned by what might go on around her.

In Uncle Charles's life there were many sadnesses. His wife Violet went mad. Christabel, Lady Aberconway has written about it in *A Wiser Woman*. She went to stay at Petworth:

I don't think it was hatred that made Lord Leconfield leave his poor wife for a year in Bedlam. It happened like this. Just before Whitsuntide she had an acute mental breakdown, and a doctor hurriedly put her into Bedlam. Apparently no one went to see her there and the doctors at Bedlam kept on saying that she was comfortable and improving. When she did improve and became almost normal again she suffered dreadfully. Her bed was too short, it twanged when she turned over, she had no bedside lamp, the ceiling light was sometimes turned off at 7 p.m., sometimes at 11 p.m. She had all her meals with the other inmates who never spoke except to say 'Pass the Marmite', and worst of all, she had nothing to read – she who was an om-nivorous reader of biographies, stories and poetry. Then she read a notice, which I believe has to be in every room in an asylum, saying that the inmate, if she or he wished, could write to the Archbishop of Canterbury or to the Lord Chancellor. She then wrote to the Lord Chancellor, Lord Jowitt. When William Jowitt received her letter, knowing that she was a friend of mine, he telephoned to me saying what an extraordinary thing it was that she should be in Bedlam, 'and', he added, 'we always send a doctor down to investigate these cases. I'll see that he goes at once.' 'Why don't you go yourself, William, and see what the place is *really* like?' I suggested, 'but don't tell them you are coming.' To his everlasting honour, busy as he was, William went. He was horrified at her plight, and at once got her a longer, silent bed, but he could not get her a bedside lamp. I suppose he must have reported her condition to Lord Lecon-field. Anyhow, within a few days she was moved to an admirable nursing home. . . .William Jowitt was the first Lord Chancellor to visit Bedlam in person for two hundred and fifty years!

We never knew why she changed her name from Violet to Violette. We just assumed, I suppose, that she was eccentric like the rest of us, only more so. Certainly the neighbours thought the same; otherwise they would not have been unkind to her. For example when she sent a telegram to her neighbour, Lord Winterton (widely known as Eddy) at Shillinglee: 'Can you come to dine at Petworth next Tuesday? Violette.' Eddy telegraphed back: 'Non, Edouard.'

Uncle Charles was a unique character and a law unto himself – and a very disciplinary law too. He ate so much that, after consultation with his physician, he decided to restrict himself to huge breakfasts and huge dinners, thus cutting out two meals, potentially huge. A baked egg and a glass of Madeira became his rule at luncheon. By the evening, quite ravenous, he would wander about the great house from room to room, staring out of rather bulbous eyes at his guests (if any), but saying nothing.

This business of not eating lunch caused him to dine on the early side. Once, when he was due to preside over a dinner of the Sussex Club in London, the organisers waited on him to discuss all the arrangements, including the time of the dinner. Uncle Charles immediately prescribed 7.30. This they thought a shade early, and they suggested 8.15 instead. To which Uncle Charles replied:

'Don't forget, some of us don't have any luncheon.' And so 7.30 it was.

It fell to Uncle Charles, as patron of the living of Petworth, to appoint a rector there. The clergyman arrived with a groom-gardener and a house-parlourmaid. This was at the beginning of the present century, and the rector's staff was for those days considered very modest. Soon after the rector had installed himself, he saw a party of woodmen preparing to cut down a yew tree in the churchyard. 'Who sent you to cut down this tree?' he inquired. Uncle Charles, they said. The rector, declaring that the business of the churchyard was his business and nobody else's, sent them away. So off they went to the Estate Office and reported what had happened to the head forester, who told it to the chief clerk, who told it to the agent, who told it to his Lordship, who wrote a note to the rector and gave it to the butler, who gave it to the first footman, who gave it to a boy who took it to the rector.

Uncle Charles's note said: 'Dear Rector, I shall be obliged if you would not interfere with my servants when they are carrying out my instructions.'

The rector wrote back: 'Thank you for your letter. I shall send round my groom-gardener and my house-parlourmaid to cut down the big cedar tree on your south lawn. I shall be grateful if you will not interfere with my servants when they are carrying out my instructions.'

Many years later, Uncle Charles was bedridden and dying, attended by a nurse in a room on the ground floor of Petworth House which is now my private dining-room. Low blood-pressure was his chief trouble – not enough blood was going through his brain to make it work properly unless he lost his temper. Otherwise he existed in a daze. Once, when I went to call on him, I found him

propped up with pillows on a truckle bed in this lower
chamber – which incidentally had been George, Lord
Egremont's bedroom a hundred years before. Various
portraits by Sir Joshua Reynolds hung around the walls,
including one of Lady Melbourne, the mother of the Prime
Minister, who (I should not be surprised) was possibly
conceived there.

George Egremont was supposed to have done all sorts
of things in that room, but I doubt if he ever did what I
found Uncle Charles doing that day. He was fishing.
Propped up on pillows, he was holding in his hand an
imaginary fishing-rod and casting an imaginary line.
'Careful, my boy,' he said as I entered, 'otherwise you
might get the hook in your ear.' I was naturally surprised.
The nurse said to me: 'Sit down out of the way for the
moment and keep quiet. He is perfectly happy.' This I did,
but I whispered to her: 'Do you know anything about
fishing? Otherwise he is likely to catch you out.' She said
to leave it to her. So the fishing went on, Uncle Charles
shouting from the bed: 'Is the line going out all right?'
and the nurse saying yes. I guessed that the nurse knew
nothing about fishing and so I feared that this harmless
exercise would not have a happy end. But as she had told
me to keep quiet, I did so.

Then Uncle Charles asked the nurse the depth of the
water. She said about two inches. He blew up. He had
been under the impression that he was fishing on the bank
of the River Derwent in Cumberland. The nurse's answer
caused a rush of blood to his brain. He suddenly realised
where he was and rounded on the nurse and me for diddling
him.

I changed the subject by talking about fox-hunting.
Uncle Charles asked if I could blow a horn. I said no, I

couldn't properly and doubted whether I ever would. Uncle Charles said: 'If you weren't so bloody blind, you might make a bloody good huntsman: I can't stand a huntsman who makes a continual noise on his horn.'

Shortly afterwards he expired.

With his death – it was in 1952 – I became the owner of the Petworth and Egremont estates and successor to some of the figures whom I have been writing about. I shall return to Petworth later – to our tussle with the Treasury over death duties and to the future of agriculture as I see it.

Meanwhile I go back a little in my own life, to the beginning of the war and to my experiences in the Private Office.

CHAPTER THREE

With Macmillan
in the Mediterranean

IN 1939 I went to Cambridge. After I had been there a year nearly all my friends had joined the armed forces, for which I myself had been turned down on the grounds of defective eyesight. I felt at a loose end and applied to go into the Civil Service.

I was accepted by the Ministry of Supply, and there I worked in a division called SS2D. The divisional head was V. P. Harries, who later became Under-Secretary at the Ministry of Aviation. Others among my colleagues were Douglas Logan, later Sir Douglas and Principal of the University of London; William Dale, later Sir William and Legal Adviser in the Commonwealth Relations Office; and R. E. Megarry, who is now a High Court Judge. They were all frighteningly clever, but they were very kind to me. I was put on to purchasing and requisitioning and entered into the task with zest, frequently having to fight Lord Beaverbrook's piratical organisation in the Ministry of Aircraft Production, who were often bent on the same object. Harries, Logan, Dale and Megarry gave me a free rein and stood up for me when I made a mess of things. I don't think that I lost much to the Ministry of Aircraft Production, but if I did we got our own back in the end, because Lord Beaverbrook became

Minister of Supply, and then the boot was on the other foot.

One day I was walking down a passage in the Ministry and just passing the Establishment Officer's door, which was ajar, when I caught the words, 'Then I am afraid it is Wyndham.' For days I was on tenterhooks. What had I done? I thought of all the reciprocal deceit which I had practised – behind my mask of innocent youth – on the Ministry of Aircraft Production. I thought of all the tiresome files that I had messed up, and I saw myself being relegated to the mines or the Pioneer Corps. But Harries, Logan, Dale and Megarry said nothing, and I was too shy to ask about it, so I kept my worries to myself.

When the Establishment Officer did send for me it was to say that I was to be the Parliamentary Secretary's private secretary. He thought that I was too young for the job, but, he said, they could think of nobody else. The Parliamentary Secretary was Harold Macmillan, whom I did not know. I said goodbye to my friends in SS2D, went to work for him, and have been devoted to Mr Macmillan ever since.

When in 1942 he was moved to the Colonial Office, as Parliamentary Under-Secretary of State, he took me with him. There he was in charge of the Economic Section. One day Mr Creasy, the Civil Service head of the section (afterwards Sir Gerald Creasy and a colonial governor), said that he was absolutely fed up because a cargo of green tea destined for one of our colonies had been pinched by the War Office, who had refused him any explanation. Dredging up such expertise as I had acquired in the Ministry of Supply from my brushes with the Ministry of Aircraft Production, I got in touch with the War Office. After a bit of trouble I was told that, if Mr Macmillan would be good enough to go round to see the Secretary of

State for War, the latter was sure that Mr Macmillan would understand, and that the whole thing would be settled amicably. Mr Macmillan stepped round and learned that the green tea was for the delectation of the Moslems of North Africa, which the Allies were about to invade.

This was the first that we knew about it, but we were soon to hear more, when the Prime Minister sent for Mr Macmillan and offered him the post of Minister Resident at Allied Force Headquarters in Algiers, with the rank of a Cabinet Minister. Mr Macmillan at once accepted, and so off we went to the Mediterranean, where for two years, following the armies across North Africa and into Italy, we moved from villa to villa.

It was New Year's Day in 1943 when we left England. Mr Macmillan was then aged forty-eight and I was twenty-two. We had two shorthand typists with us, and that was all. The Foreign Office had planned to send out Roger Makins as Mr Macmillan's chief adviser, but we set off before he could be ready. Learning that we had gone without a keeper, the Foreign Office hastily sent Pierson Dixon after us, who arrived hot-foot to find us in the Aletti Hotel in Algiers.

I see that in writing to my parents a week or so later I call Mr Macmillan 'Uncle Harold'. I wonder if I started a trend among official staffs who become fond of their masters?

10.1.43

Dearest Mamma,

This is the first chance I've had of writing to you – and I've got it because today is Sunday and Uncle Harold has gone to church. I have remained in bed at our hotel, and I don't propose to get up until I reckon the parson is half-way through his sermon.

It is a lovely day with bright sun and clear sky: Algiers is looking its best with the white houses reflecting the sunshine and the Mediterranean – fifty yards from me as I write – is a deep blue. The spectacle is such that no visiting foreigner could regret his advent to these parts.

All that is what the *femme de chambre* says. I cannot see for myself, because the air-raids have blown the glass out of my bedroom window, and the management has stopped it up with pasteboard. I've got the electric light on, and it might be midnight in Manchester so far as I am concerned.

We had a good journey out – in a Hudson bomber. We flew from Hendon to an airfield in Cornwall, where we lunched and kicked our heels in the officers' mess, or dossed in a hut, until 2 a.m., when we breakfasted off bacon and eggs, were wished a happy New Year and left England.

At Government House, Gibraltar, our fellow guests were Lord Gort, who without warning had turned up from Malta in a Beaufighter, and a professor on a visit from the British Council offices in Madrid.

Algiers now is, I imagine, in many ways like the great base ports in France in the last war. Administrative officers of all ranks and services abound. Boots and spurs protrude from under office desks. But whereas there huts were provided for much of the influx, here existing buildings are made to suffice. More and more quarts get crammed into the pint pot. Life is very cheek-by-jowl in a town the population of which had already increased by 50 per cent in the last three years without a compensating increase in housing.

For our first forty-eight hours here my bedroom had to serve as the ministerial office. Many an historic personality has expressed admiration of my scarlet pyjamas.

We have now got a proper office. I hope we shall be established soon in a house by ourselves. In the meantime we eat in a naval mess where, needless to say, we are treated very hospitably.

F

I have brought two books out with me; but at the rate Uncle Harold is running me I shall probably bring them both back to England at the end of this mission with the pages uncut.

Makins hasn't turned up yet. The Foreign Office has sent out a man called Bob Dixon to fill his place until he arrives.

It is not for me to say it – but Uncle Harold is being a great success. He is much liked, his sincerity is admired, and he has made constructive suggestions which have been hungrily welcomed.

I don't know when we shall be out of this wood and back in England again. In the meantime it is a very stimulating wood to be in. But there are an awful lot of trees.

Best love from

JOHN

During the month, President Roosevelt and Mr Churchill met in conference at Casablanca.

Robert Murphy, then the American Political Representative in North Africa, has explained that when the United States agreed to send an expedition to Africa, the American plan was to conduct merely a brief campaign to expel the Germans and Italians from that continent, and afterwards – without delay – to invade Europe from bases in the British Isles. But the British were determined to invade Europe first from the south. Before the opening of the Casablanca conference (actually at the nearby town of Anfa) Mr Churchill had said that we were not to hurry the Americans or to try to force agreement – we should take plenty of time. The British advised what they called a compromise, proposing that after Africa was cleared, Sicily should be occupied by an Anglo-American force in order to assure a relatively safe shipping route through the Mediterranean. Although the compromise was adopted, the American High Command never changed its outlook: as Mr Murphy saw it, 'For the two years we fought there, we were a reluctant tail to the British kite, and thus failed to exploit several opportunities.'

Robert Murphy admired Mr Macmillan, as we know from his book *Diplomat Among Warriors*:

We got along famously together. . . . Macmillan's official title in Algiers was Minister Resident, so President Roosevelt elevated me to ministerial rank to match his status. Macmillan was not a career diplomat, nor did he bring to Algiers any exceptional knowledge of French or African affairs. What he did bring was exceptional common sense and knowledge of British politics. Churchill wrote Roosevelt that one reason he chose Macmillan was because, like Churchill himself, he had an American mother. But no American would suspect that ancestry. Macmillan – in dignity, voice, manners, dress, and personality – was and still is almost the American popular image of an English gentleman. . . . His political weight in London was vastly greater than mine in Washington, but I cannot recall a single instance when he invoked this to swing the balance of opinion at Allied Force Headquarters.

Macmillan's assignment in Algiers required more delicate diplomacy than mine did. He had to avoid the appearance of untoward influence, not only upon military leaders, but upon Americans of every kind. Churchill also was careful not to draw attention to his personal representative. Even after the war was long over, Churchill listed Macmillan in the index of his war memoirs as 'assistant to the American political representative North Africa' – that is, me. According to one story which circulated in Algiers during the war, Macmillan told his British staff: 'These Americans represent the new Roman Empire and we Britons, like the Greeks of old, must teach them how to make it go.' Whether or not he ever spoke such words during his service in Algiers, he did indeed exercise greater influence upon Anglo-American affairs in the Mediterranean than was generally recognised.

For one thing, Macmillan's government kept him better

informed than my government did me. More than once I learned
first from Macmillan and other British colleagues of decisions
taken in Washington of vital importance to our joint enterprises.
This was not a personal matter but a defect in Washington's
co-ordination. The British Foreign Office cabled duplicates of
relevant reports to all its representatives concerned. When I
complained that I had to depend upon the British to keep up to
date with what was happening in Washington, the reply came
that the State Department could not afford the expensive British
procedure. That explanation sounded ironic, coming at a time
when the British Government was frankly bankrupt and was
getting billions in Lend-Lease from the United States. But the
finances of the State Department were subject to the discretion
of congressional committees.

I wrote home :

30.1.43

Dearest Mamma,

I've had two letters from you – the two that came with Roger
[Makins]. But we hope the Bag Service will improve shortly.

Uncle Harold's come back in good form from the Anfa
Conference. I did not go with him there, but it seems to have
been a striking, if utility, field of the Cloth of Gold.

Old Mr Will Codrington from Preston is staying with us at
present. He came along from Anfa where he had been employed
in connection with the conference. About the only person I've
come across out here whom I had seen before is Hugh Fraser.

But we are nicely off for Prime Ministers' sons. Randolph
Churchill and Lord Corvedale [son of Baldwin] are frequently
on our doorstep.

I seem to have spent most of this last week doing little else
but equip the Ministerial villa. There is hardly anything to be
bought in the town; but the Navy and Army have been very
good to us, always ready with loans.

Our kitchen battery we got by an S.O.S. to Gibraltar.

The French and Arab servants at the villa say to me :

'Oui, Monsieur le Sécretaire,' whenever I tell them anything

We've not had General Eisenhower to dinner yet, so I've never seen him. He is no doubt a man with praiseworthy sentiments; and he expresses them in an arresting manner. 'Christ on the mountain, Minister,' he ejaculated earnestly when Uncle Harold last called on him: 'I'm idealistic as hell!'

Who says we and the Americans talk the same language?

All my love to you

JOHN

Mr Churchill passed through Algiers after the Casablanca conference.

13.2.43

Dearest Mamma,

There is little leisure here. When the day's work is finished, the evening's entertaining begins. Americans, Frenchmen, Englishmen, are summoned to dinner and stay until bedtime. The private secretary nourishes his strength on quarts of Algerian wine.

The household staff I've collected is a cosmopolitan and varied crew. The cook is a Dutchman (naturalised English) and a private in the Army Catering Corps; there are two soldier servants (a gunner and a grenadier), a Spanish–French housemaid, an Arab, a Negro, a security policeman who hails from Norwich, and a military driver who in peace-time was a racing motorbicyclist.

The P.M. when he passed through here stayed with Admiral Cunningham. Something went wrong with his aeroplane and he got held up for a day, a large part of which he spent working in bed. Old Giraud came round to see him. He nipped out of bed, put on his siren-suit and then, as he had a slight cold, he donned an enormous flowered silk dressing-gown, with his few old hairs standing on end, he welcomed the General.

He went off, I am told, in terrific form with an overcoat covering the garb described above, and enquiring as he got into the aeroplane whether the dressing gown showed. Of course it did.

Last night there was a private showing of some American propaganda film. I went along with Uncle Harold and Roger. While I was standing about inside the entrance of the cinema a Frenchman approached me. He was the eldest son of the Vaudoyers, the family I lived with in Paris. His father and mother are, so far as he knows, still there. He hasn't heard from them for a year. He himself was taken prisoner fighting the Germans, escaped, and is now a reporter for a local news agency here.

I hope to go up next week with Uncle Harold to visit General Anderson's army.

Air Marshal Tedder has arrived in Algiers, and who should he have in tow but the ubiquitous Lord Forbes. The latter is coming to see me, I think tomorrow, to borrow knives and forks for the Marshal's table.

It would be very nice if, some time, you could wrap up a book and send it to me in the Bag. A volume or two of *The Decline and Fall* would be very welcome. Please don't bother much about it, but if you should happen to see a cheap edition in a shop I should be very grateful if you would remember me. There are few good books of any kind in this barren town. I've only got one book at the moment, but as it is *War and Peace* and as there aren't many chances of reading, I shall be all right for a bit.

Peyrouton, the Governor General, has just been to lunch. You will have heard in London of his reported political blemishes. As regards his personal characteristics, his features have led us to nickname him Tiberius; his conversation is decked with a suave wit, and its analogies are drawn largely from the realm of '*l'amour*', nor, I should think, are they based on hearsay.

All my love to you

JOHN

My letters home were the letters of a very young man, and in many respects they may now look pretty ingenuous. But however naïve they may seem more than twenty years later, they are at least an authentic if modest record of the time, of small importance against the backcloth of great events but providing, all the same, a footnote. I was there, and I was an onlooker and sometimes a participant. These are the notes of one witness.

I feel myself that the letters may have a certain social interest. Perhaps they convey some flavour of a society now greatly changed.

Be that as it may, we soon had a very efficient little office for the Resident Minister in Algiers. Roger Makins was the head, and two other members were Harold Caccia and Anthony Rumbold. I doubt whether any foreign mission in peace or war has ever contained so much ability concentrated in so few people. At first I was just a wide-eyed onlooker, but I hope a willing learner. Busy though they were, my new colleagues still found time to educate me in tasks for which I had no training. They were very kind and forbearing to me, but it must have been a bit of a bind for them.

At this time we were rather bothered about a French Admiral called Godfroy, who was in Alexandria Harbour in command of a French naval squadron which had been there ever since the fall of France. Admiral Godfroy and his squadron were not causing us any trouble. The trouble was that Admiral Godfroy wasn't causing anybody any trouble. He was sitting there with his squadron as a non-combatant. It was therefore proposed that Mr Macmillan and a French Admiral who had come over to the Allied side should fly to Egypt from Algiers above the German lines and exercise persuasion on Admiral Godfroy. Mr Macmillan agreed, and asked me to go with him, 'though' he said to me glumly, 'I should imagine the whole squadron is by now grounded on its own empties.'

We set off at midnight in a bomber – Mr Macmillan,

the French Admiral, the Admiral's Flag Lieutenant and myself. It was a British bomber, so I did the honours: after a bit of *après-vous* business, Mr Macmillan got in first and went and sat beside the pilot, the Admiral got in next, and then the Flag Lieutenant and myself. The bomber took off and almost immediately crashed in flames in a vineyard close to the airfield.

Being by the door, I opened it and got out, followed by the Admiral with his hat on fire, the Flag Lieutenant, and the crew. I was only bruised and shaken, but I had lost my spectacles. Not being able to see very much, I asked whether Mr Macmillan was one of us lying in the vineyard beside the blazing plane. To my horror they said no. My God, what was I to do? Dive into the burning plane and perish with my master in the flames – a sort of private secretarial suttee? Or win the George Cross by rescuing him – a seemingly impossible task? Or spend the rest of my life in shame for having got myself out without him? Suddenly a familiar figure was seen to be struggling to get out of the pilot's side-window, his moustache burning with a bright blue flame. He was quite out of reach. We shouted: 'Push, Minister, push.' He landed on the ground with a thump, very badly burnt.

On and off, I have worked for Mr Macmillan for some twenty years, and I can truthfully say that I have never in my life given him a lead except when it came to getting out of that aeroplane. He himself has described his escape with typical humour: 'Middle-aged and rather portly publishers,' as he put it, 'encumbered by the weight of their own dignity and a large green Ulster overcoat, trying to spring through a smallish hole . . . over . . . mechanical devices of a jagged and impeding kind . . . must be inspired by a powerful and overwhelming motive.' For lesser exertions, he said, such as to enter Parliament, or to struggle through years of political failure and frustration, lesser motives might serve. Ambition, patriotism, pride – all these might impel a man and finally bring him within the hallowed precincts of the Privy Council and the Cabinet. But, he said, for what he did in the early hours of that morning, only one motive in the world was sufficient: 'Fear, (not fame) is the spur.'

Mr Macmillan is a brave man. He was always getting us into scrapes, sometimes I thought unnecessarily. Once when he was proposing that some of us should join him in a dangerous expedition I ventured to suggest that our presence was unnecessary, not to say risky. We must go all the same, he replied, so I said that if the worst came to the worst the cry would be 'Wyndham and children first!' Whenever we got into a fix thereafter the blessed Minister would shout 'Wyndham and children first!' The cry has haunted me ever since.

The war in North Africa proceeded according to the grand design. The Allied armies from Egypt and Algeria were to meet each other and throw the Germans and Italians out of North Africa; which they did, and then invaded Italy with much difficulty but great success. If only so many troops had not been withdrawn from Italy in 1944, the Allied armies might have gone on into Central Europe from Italy. So many were taken away for landings in the South of France, which turned out to be a walkover, that Field-Marshal Alexander was prevented from pouring armies through the Ljubljana gap and thence reaching Vienna. It was a great pity. What the British tried to achieve at the Casablanca conference was confounded in the end. But that we could not know then. For myself, I went about my private secretarial duties in Algiers.

Dearest Mamma,

I am sitting on the airfield, about six miles outside Algiers, waiting for Lord Gort. He is coming over for a short visit from Malta, and I have motored out to meet him. Nobody has been quite sure exactly when the aeroplane will get here, so I have brought out a writing pad.

It's a hot windless day. I am at the base of the Control Tower. Before me is the airfield : in January it was a sea of mud, now it is an expanse of dust. To the west lie Algiers and the coastal plain. To the east rise the mountains. Over the mountains will come winging Lord Gort.

In the meantime here is a good opportunity for writing to you.

We took Uncle Harold out into the country on Sunday where we had a picnic lunch. Hardly had we sat down to our meal when an offensive youth appeared on the scene and said did we realise we were on private property. An altercation took place and he went off to fetch his uncle whose property it was. The uncle arrived fat and fierce with a bristling moustache and the whole of his household (8 persons). We began to feel a bit uncomfortable. But when the old fellow learnt we were English all was smiles, a bottle of wine was fetched, the success of the Allies was drunk and so on. It transpired that we had been suspected of being parachutists.

We came to a great tomb on a hill. It was built in a beehive shape with Doric columns round the base. An old Arab, who was standing by, said it had been built before the Arab invasion. General Catroux, who came to dinner that night, said it had housed the remains of Cleopatra's daughter. But I have not had a chance to find out about it myself.

God bless my soul, here comes Lord Gort.

Saw Lord Gort off. What a nice and modest Field-Marshal! I took him for walks and lost the way but he never complained. He asked after my father.

This afternoon went back to the airfield to see off General Catroux, bound for London.

This evening I had hoped to have to myself, for Uncle Harold and Roger were both dining out; but at about five the R.A.F. telephoned to say that Sir Charles Woolley, Governor of Cyprus, had landed *en route* for Cyprus from London, that he would be here for five hours and would I take him off their hands. I trundled out to the airfield once more and did.

A funny sort of day ended with Sir Charles, sustained by the local plum brandy playing 'I'll walk beside thee' on our piano. He's gone now and I'm alone.

All my love to you

JOHN

P.S. Guess what. Eric Duncannon has been appointed to our staff.

Lord Duncannon, now Lord Bessborough, who spoke French so well because his mother was French, was a helpful addition to our small office.

2.5.43

Dearest Mamma,

Uncle Harold and I are at an inn called the Hôtel de Rivage in a village on the shore of the Mediterranean about 40 miles from Algiers. Tipasa is the village. We came here yesterday (Saturday) because Uncle Harold said he wanted a change. Inland, about two miles away, rise high and rocky hills. Between there and the sea are vineyards. Under a cliff, in a bay, is the village and a harbour : a few houses, and a customs house and a sleepy post-office with a rather tattered flag hanging over the door.

The inn is small and bare but clean – run by an old couple, a boy and two Arab women.

The village seems at first just a fishing-village and nothing more. But mount the cliff behind the inn and you get a thrill. Over a large area, half hidden by wild flowers and shrubs are the remains of a great Roman town which must have contained about 40,000 people. Forum, theatre (in which Uncle Harold recited an unconscionable amount of Greek verse to test the acoustics), market, Christian church are all to be distinguished. Work has of course been pursued by archaeologists; but the flowers and trees have not been torn out, and I hope they never will be. The effect of this dead city in a wild garden between the hills and the sea can be imagined.

We were struck by a misty-blue shrub and wondered what it was until we were told ladies in France used a similar plant to scent their cupboards. So it must have been wild lavender.

This morning we went out after breakfast and walked westward between the hills and the Mediterranean. Soon the hills swallowed up the foreshore plain and dropped sheer and rocky to the sea. We pursued our path along a kind of corniche track. We kept on prolonging our walk to see what the next bend in the track would reveal. This tantalising occupation and the splendour of the view led us many miles, in fact between 15 and 20.

I write this in the garden of the inn waiting to return to Algiers.

Algiers – that evening.

The weather in Algiers is worse – the locals say – than it has been at this season for many years. For several days there have been heavy grey skies, rain, and on the top of the cliff where we live, a hanging cloud. A man who left here a fortnight ago for a short trip to England departed quite pale and returned today bronzed, saying he was sorry to be late but he'd had a touch of the sun when staying with a friend in Dorset. We were most envious. If you imagine us under the proverbial African sky, you should come and spend a day or two with us here in our cloud.

The gardener attributes this misty weather – erroneously – to the smoke-screen apparatus which forms part of our anti-aircraft defences. But the Spanish housemaid – a more simple soul – says the *bon Dieu* has sent it along to keep the English from feeling homesick.

Our latest guest has been a Mr Jones, the New Zealand

Minister of Defence. His private secretary lost all their papers on the way here and I had a bad time finding them again, finally running them to ground in Gibraltar.

We've got a Russian mission coming to lunch tomorrow, so I am laying on gallons of spirits.

Best love from

JOHN

We made a visit to London for consultations in May of 1943.

5.6.43

Dearest Mamma,

On the journey back here General Bonseat's A.D.C. was sick among us all before the aircraft had been three quarters of an hour in the air.

Algiers has been hectic since our return.

I was sent out to represent Uncle Harold at de Gaulle's arrival. At first it was intended that the General should come to an airfield called Maison Blanche; but later the choice was changed to one called Boufarik, about fifteen miles from Maison Blanche. As I missed the message informing me of this change I went to Maison Blanche. *Ventre à terre* would hardly describe my subsequent progress over the fifteen miles to Boufarik, for the car nearly flew, and we did it in twenty minutes. The scene was a very small landing-ground in a fertile plain : vineyards, olive groves, ripened crops all around, and the mountains as usual embellishing the sky-line. A little group of Frenchmen headed by old Giraud stood with the docile expectancy of beasts awaiting the judges at a county show, while surrounding them crowded the Press, fulfilling the role of spectators, in a holiday mood. A side-show was provided by a guard of honour sweating profusely in the midday heat. A statement by Giraud was handed round among the journalists. Eric Duncannon, who had turned up to see the fun and to take my place should I fail to arrive in time, obliged with a translation of it into English.

De Gaulle came out of the sky in a machine marked 'Paris'. The two generals shook hands : '*Bonjour, mon général.*' '*Bonjour, de Gaulle.*' The latter gave the guard of honour the once-over, shook hands with the attendant Frenchmen, was invited to say a few words into a microphone, declined, and got into a car with Giraud and Catroux. We all swept back to Algiers at at least sixty miles an hour.

This brisk meeting was followed by days in which rumours were rife, all sorts of things were prophesied, hoped and feared.

But now at last the united [French] committee has been formed. Touch wood.

Best love from

JOHN

8.6.43

Dearest Mamma,

I am writing this waiting to meet a visitor at the airfield again. The paper comes from Driver Pocklington's notebook.

As I expect you've discovered, we had the P.M. and Mr Eden in Algiers. They had a press conference in our new garden – I set up a running buffet for the reporters ; so our hard-won stocks of liquor are rather depleted now.

Our driver Pocklington got a raspberry from the P.M. about something that wasn't his fault when he was driving the visitors. Mr Eden said not to worry about it. Pocklington replied stoutly that on the contrary he regarded it as an honour : few people could say they'd been ticked off by the P.M. 'Don't you believe it!' said Mr Eden feelingly.

This airfield is baking, with dust flying about. It is a Clapham Junction of the Near East. In the short time I've been waiting, I've seen a Colonel from Cairo, an American civilian from Tunis, a naval officer from Malta, a flock of people from Tripoli, a Frenchman from Morocco. There is a chauffeur alongside waiting to meet a man from Bathurst. And my visitor is coming from Gibraltar.

I went to church yesterday. The sermon was about St Paul's visit to Athens and the Stoics and Epicureans and the business of the altar to the unknown god. When we got outside an English officer said to an American, 'I suppose you chaps think a Stoic is a bird what brings babies?'

Best love from

JOHN

De Gaulle, shortly after his arrival in Algiers, came to call on Mr Macmillan in our horrible but highly efficient office in the Rue Professeur Curtillet. I met De Gaulle at the street door. He advanced towards the lift, but I had to advise him not to get into it. The lift, I explained, was unreliable – we had already had two Field-Marshals stuck in it. So we mounted the stairs, and I showed him into Harold Macmillan's room, where Mr Macmillan greeted him. De Gaulle surveyed our dingy surroundings with the eye of an heir who was about to succeed, and asked like a prospective landlord, although it was nothing to do with him : '*On est bien ici?*'

But very soon after this a great deal was to do with General de Gaulle. About six o'clock one morning Robert Murphy received a telephone call asking him to go round to French Headquarters. Murphy was used to early morning calls from this source because Giraud normally began his day at 4.30 a.m. A typically unfunny joke of Giraud's was that the difference between generals and diplomats was that generals rose very early to do nothing all day, while diplomats rose very late for the same purpose. When Murphy arrived at Giraud's office he was shown several decrees which Giraud had signed. He saw at once that Giraud had unwittingly, but to the intents and purposes of others, signed away all his powers to de Gaulle. Giraud was astonished when Murphy put this to him. 'But I was never told that!' he declared. Then, after a moment's reflection, he shrugged his shoulders and said that it had nothing to do with Murphy.

That was the end of Giraud. De Gaulle took over. Giraud was relieved of his command.

In Algiers there was such a cloak-and-dagger atmosphere that one came to regard it as normal, and we had some rather hair-raising experiences.

I remember that some ingenious people had invented an explosive disguised as animals' droppings – camel-dung for deserts, cowpats for Southern Europe, and so forth. They were all very pleased with their work. A man whose duty it was to interest other servants of the Crown in this stuff, and who was obviously keen, told me that he could provide almost any kind of explosive dung. He had a very good line in elephant pats – 'enormous and very lethal'. I had to tell him that elephants in the Mediterranean area had gone out with Hannibal. We settled for cow- and camel-pats.

We eagerly awaited the first consignment, but unhappily it blew up in transit in a neutral country, blasting the roof off a customs shed. The courier kept his head, however, and – his face blackened with gunpowder – rushed round to the British Consul-General. There he was, he said, a British subject going about his harmless business, when all his luggage had been destroyed by an explosion in the Customs shed. This was not the sort of thing that he was prepared to put up with, and what was the Consul-General going to do about it? A protest was lodged. The matter was never resolved – a result with which we ourselves were very satisfied.

Well, they tried it again, and this time the courier arrived successfully, equipped with cowpats and camel-pats. But we never did find out who got the labels mixed up. An enemy squadron of tanks in an African desert were astonished to find a lot of cowpats there. Men got out, and having prodded them were blown up. About the same time the enemy were amazed to find a camel-pat on a railway bridge in Southern Europe. The situation was investigated with similar results : bridge and all went up.

With the capture of Tunisia I had to think about setting up a small branch office for Mr Macmillan in Tunis. Our armies had taken about 240,000 prisoners, many of whom came walking into Tunis to give themselves up, for they had no hope otherwise. There were some rather surprising scenes. One day an Artillery officer, the present Lord Camrose, was going along a road on the outskirts of Tunis when he met a body of Germans, all heavily armed. Now I'm for it, he thought. But they explained that they just wanted to know the way to a post office where they could send letters off to their families before they gave themselves up.

The prisoners were very helpful and co-operative. They were given the materials and constructed prisoners' cages, into which, when built, they went. We let them keep their bands, who cheered them up by playing jolly German tunes.

I had gone up to Tunis by car, and it took me two days. I started with a box full of rations, a sergeant clerk and a driver. On the first day we lost the rations. The sergeant managed to drop them in a pond where we had stopped for lunch. As we pursued our journey, there was a marked coolness between my two military companions, which, however, I was able to relieve by making several halts and by fair means or normal repairing the loss.

We spent the night in a field behind a farm in the hills near the city of Constantine. The farmer was a fairly prosperous Moslem in European clothes and lived with a not unattractive French woman whom the farm hands called Mademoiselle. They had a fair-haired khaki-coloured son aged five. Mademoiselle was very shy; but she cooked me a dinner and gave me wine and a home-made liqueur which made me feel as if my inside was on fire.

The next night we spent behind another farm in a grove of almond trees. The farm buildings were battle-scarred, and among the trees was the wreckage of a German lorry and an anti-tank gun. I found an Italian family in the farm: an old man, a young man and his wife, and two other women. They were naturally anxious to oblige and had plenty to say in Italian. I made polite gestures and took some water from their well to wash in.

Arrived in Tunis, I found myself in a large empty house which had formerly been occupied by the British Consul-General. General Alexander, then commanding XV Army Group, had one part of it, and I took over another. The house had been given to Queen Victoria by a nineteenth-century Bey of Tunis in a naïve and abortive attempt to counteract the French intrusion.

General Alexander and his staff, who were planning the invasion of Sicily, lived in tents in the garden and in neighbouring fields, but they came indoors for meals, which they had on a covered terrace. Everything about that General's Headquarters was clean, orderly and austere, but – like the great General himself – very human, calm and civilised. The General invited me to be a member of his mess, an invitation which I gratefully accepted, though, as a young and most unmilitary civilian, with some trepidation. I was afraid that they would all be talking about the war, and that I should feel quite out of it. But what happened? I was most courteously welcomed by the General, and at dinner I sat next to his Military Secretary, Colonel Lord William Scott. The conversation was like good conversation in a good country house. I remember the subjects covered, and this is what they were:

1. Lord Winterton (who with Mr Shinwell had been needling the Government in the House of Commons – they were called at the time Arsenic and Old Lace).
2. Whales.
3. Cardinal Wolsey's breath.
4. How King Frederick I of Prussia recruited his guards.
5. The best way to exterminate rabbits.
6. How to make deer-keeping pay.
7. The antecedents of the Duke of Buccleuch's huntsman.

They were all very good to me. I slept wrapped in blankets in a huge and empty marble hall. Marble is rather chilly stuff to sleep on.

Mr Macmillan came up with Harold Caccia, and for our return journey to Algiers General Alexander lent him his comfortable aeroplane. As the aircraft was about to take off, a tyre burst, but we were not going very fast, and no further damage occurred. We all got out a trifle shaken, however. I nipped up to the control tower and found that there was a courier aircraft taxi-ing to take off for Algiers. I had it stopped. There was just room for two, so Mr Macmillan and Harold Caccia boarded it and flew off perched rather uncomfortably on their luggage, indicating to me that I had better follow them as best I could. I did so next morning alone in the Commander-in-Chief's aeroplane, which had to go to Algiers for maintenance. The captain flew low to show me everything of interest on the way.

30.8.43

Dearest Mamma,

General Alexander came to stay not long ago for a night. I took him and his A.D.C. bathing. He insisted on doing so naked, which is, of course, the best way. Some F.A.N.Y.s had accordingly to be removed from the beach, and retired to the building where they were accommodated, about 100 yards away. Those who watched the proceedings from the window must have been awe-struck by the scene: the fine figure of the general, the tanned body of his American A.D.C., and stalking along, the last of the trio, a very *affairé* skeleton, me. But I dare say their eyes didn't really come out on sticks until the A.D.C. stood on his head in four feet of water.

Uncle Harold has the kindest of hearts. The other night at about 4 o'clock in the morning we had one of our occasional air-raids. I was, as usual, sleeping on the roof. I woke up and made off to one of the bedrooms downstairs and went to sleep again. The cabinet minister in his room, I learnt later, also woke up, and got out of his comfortable bed and ranged about in his pyjamas to make sure that 'that boy wasn't still fast asleep in the open upstairs.'

The Gibbon volumes you so wonderfully got for me are great fun.

Best love from

JOHN

Sicily having been captured, there was much secret to-ing and fro-ing between us and the Italians over an armistice. The Italians released a prisoner of war, General Carton de Wiart, to go to England for them with propositions. They could not have chosen a better person, except that the General, a gallant and romantic character, was well known and also conspicuous because he had only one arm, one leg and one eye. We in North Africa were worried that his arrival in England would give rise to speculation as to why he had so suddenly turned up. Nevertheless the secret was kept. A member of Mr Macmillan's staff, Tom Dupree, meanwhile paid a surreptitious visit to Lisbon where, by arrangement, he got the German line of battle. Two Italian officers came to Algiers, and finally it was arranged for the armistice discussions to take place in Sicily, the whole of which we now occupied.

At 6 a.m. on 30 August Mr Macmillan, Mr Murphy, the American representative, and General Bedell Smith, General Eisenhower's Chief of Staff, left North Africa secretly for Sicily in a small aeroplane which took four and a half hours to get there. I went with them in my accustomed capacity of ubiquitous factotum. From the opposite direction and in equal secrecy Italian envoys also arrived in Sicily. The discussions took place in a small tented camp hidden in an olive grove not far from Syracuse. There we sat for four days until an armistice was arranged. General Alexander clinched it by a purposely dramatic intervention.

The Italians had annoyed everybody else by saying that they had not been empowered to sign any surrender terms before the Allied landings on the mainland. We were not going to put up with this sort of procrastination. General Alexander, who had been waiting in reserve until he was needed, in a tent in the olive grove, now donned his best uniform with breeches and boots and prepared to intervene. There was some deliberation as to how he had best make his entrance. It was thought that he should not be seen

approaching the conference tent plodding across the
stubble, threading his way through the olive trees, and
possibly tripping over the guy-ropes of the other tents.
The situation called for panache. It was therefore decided
that he should drive up very grandly, surrounded by his
beribboned staff. So they all climbed over a wall at the back
of the camp, dusted themselves down, got into the General's
car and zoomed round to the front of the camp, arriving at
the conference tent in great style. It was a scene which I
shall never forget, as the General walked into the tent.
This handsome, gallant, gentle Alexander had a presence
which could never fail to impress. The atmosphere in the
tent, where all the bickering had been going on, changed at
once. The General dominated the scene. He greeted the
Italians with icy politeness, but did not shake hands. He
then gave them a talking-to which made me think that if I
were one of his officers and had done something wrong,
and he had spoken to me like this, I would have gone out
and shot myself. In a cold fury, but without raising his
voice, he told the Italians that if they did not stop messing
about we would bomb Rome. The General added that the
envoys would not be permitted to leave until they had
signed. They signed. At the time of the signature I was
sitting under a tree outside, and I remembered that it was
the anniversary of the declaration of war in 1939.

After that I went back to Tunis, where whom should I
find but my brother Mark, who was serving in the 12th
Lancers. He had been wounded in the desert for the second
time and had now arrived to rejoin his regiment.

29.9.43

Dearest Mamma,

It has been raining, so life is a little cooler.

I flew up here [to Tunis] last Thursday in a shower with the rain bang-banging on the outside of the aircraft and the sea looking glaucous and not at all its traditional deep-blue Mediterranean self.

It's nice to get away from Algiers on these trips from time to time – to escape the hurly-burly and bickerings and those bloody dinner-parties.

Uncle Harold had preceded me.

My arrival was on well-worn lines. 'Well,' they said, 'have you brought the butter and the whisky from Algiers?'

'Oh goodness, I forgot.'

Imprecations.

When that was over they announced that they had got a surprise for me. I couldn't guess what.

Five minutes later in walked the surprise. Mark. He was in great form despite the fact that he had got up at 2 a.m. that morning to make his start from Cairo. He stayed for two days, after which I took him over to a rest camp his regiment has eleven miles from here, and thence he departed to the main quarters about 200 miles further on. It was wonderful seeing him. He is going to be *perfectly safe* for quite a long time yet, I think, and I hope to see quite a lot of him in the coming months.

Uncle Harold has gone off again, but I have stayed on to take over and fix up part of the Consul-General's house as a flat-cum-office for us to use on future visits to Tunis.

We are having a crazy time putting the place right, as it had become very dilapidated. The plumber came round and was mystified by a large pipe, on the outside of the house, the lower part of which had broken off. He could not discover whether this pipe should still form an integral part of the plumbing or whether it was obsolete; so we went round turning on taps to see if water would flow out. It didn't. Until the Consul-General's maid remembered a long-forgotten, dust-laden lavatory in some dark and distant corner and entered and tried the plug, which, curiously worked; whereupon the plumber, who had been peering up the pipe, poked his head, sopping wet, round the back door and cried cheerfully up the stairs : '*Ça y est, ça y est.*'

I am writing this on a balcony looking westward across the Tunisian plain to the mountains. There is a most lovely sunset scattering scarlet on clouds which dissolve in a curtain of rain and mist over those hills. I shall be up there tomorrow, flying back to Algiers in a courier plane, perched on mail-bags.

All my love

JOHN

Finally the Italian armistice was announced after having been kept secret for several weeks. It coincided with the Allied landings on the mainland of Italy, and with an abortive attempt to make an airborne landing in the neighbourhood of Rome.

Back in Algiers, we received an excited telegram from the Prime Minister about a broadcast from Bari in which the King of Italy was referred to as King of Albania and Emperor of Ethiopia. Mr Churchill asked how the King of Italy would like to be sent back to either of those places now. I was able to find out that the broadcast was about currency and the rates of exchange and that our own people had written the text. The Italians, without meaning any harm, had simply out of habit inserted the customary heading for their proclamations. This we explained, with assurances that we would have the Italian equivalent of H.M. Stationery Office bring themselves up to date, and Mr Churchill was satisfied.

Field-Marshal Smuts now arrived in Algiers one morning, *en route* for England, and we went out to meet him at the airport. I was much impressed by this gay, brave, bright old philosopher, so full of curiosity and so ready with his views. He never stopped talking, but it was a joy to listen to him, even when he betrayed some ignorance of the complications of modern warfare. He had a bee in his bonnet. Our Middle East campaign had been conducted with conspicuous vigour and success, he thought, but he sensed a tardiness in our subsequent operations. He had the feeling that the scale and speed of our land operations now left much to be desired. The old man did not fully understand the tremendous planning involved in another leap forward.

After luncheon, at which Smuts in great good humour had teased all the Americans and British present, it was my duty to point out to him that it was time for him to leave for the airport. Smuts turned to Mr Macmillan and said: 'Why don't you come too, and then we can go on with our talk?' By then, we were all familiar with Mr Macmillan's zest, so it was scarcely a surprise when, at a moment's notice, we were off to England with Smuts, travelling thousands of miles so that the two of them could finish their conversation.

About this time the Russians started to arrive in Algiers and set up a mission with a Mr Bogomolov, an ex-Professor of Marxist Philosophy, at its head. I liked Bogomolov. When he was due to pay his first official call on Mr Macmillan, who happened to be unwell and in bed, I went round to his house to pick him up. Bogomolov looked me up and down and said nothing for quite some time until, nearing Mr Macmillan's house, he asked: '*Est-ce que vous étiez à Eton, monsieur?*' I answered: '*Oui, excellence.*' To which he replied: '*Ah, quelle jolie école.*' Praise indeed from the ex-Professor of Marxist Philosophy. But perhaps he was referring to the architecture.

16.10.43

Dearest Mamma,

Admiral Cunningham has just left to be First Sea Lord after having been C. in C. Mediterranean. He took up his command in the dark days : he lays it down having purged the Mediterranean and secured the Italian fleet in the harbour of Malta.

It was just like General Eisenhower that, when Admiral Cunningham quitted his office in Allied Force Headquarters for the last time, there was drawn up outside the building as a surprise and a courtesy a great guard of honour of all services and of both nations to salute him. And when the Admiral was to fly away this afternoon General Eisenhower had arranged for another guard of about 300 men of the British and American armies, navies and air forces and the colours of both countries and an American Marine band to be beside the Admiral's Liberator.

Mark has turned up and came in to Algiers for dinner last night, having got hold of the Orderly Room truck. He brought two brother officers called Michael de Piro and John Stimpson and we went and took dinner off Eric Duncannon on account of he has a very good cook. It is a very happy coincidence having Mark so near and I shall see a lot of him.

Best love from

JOHN

On my flying visit to London I had missed my father, who was then serving in the North of England.

To Col. The Hon. Edward Wyndham, D.S.O.

20.10.43

My dear Daddy,

Thank you for the letter you wrote to me while I was in England. It was tantalising being there and yet not seeing you; but as we came at such short notice I hadn't much hope. The trip was fixed up between Uncle Harold and Smuts while they were lunching together. At 2.30 the same afternoon we were in the air.

The biggest event here lately has been the arrival of Mark. He is about 15 miles away.

Colonel Oliver Stanley came through today on the way home

from a tour of some of his Colonial Empire. From the point of view of a private secretary he was a perfect guest. He arrived after breakfast and left before lunch, so there was no entertaining to be organised; he asked few questions; he complained neither of the heat nor of the dust; he adhered to his original plans. If there was a hitch it was only that a retired admiral in the Colonial Secretary's entourage called Bromley had lost his teeth in the aircraft on the way when they had happened upon an air-pocket, and we had to have some of the fittings in the cabin unscrewed before they could be retrieved.

The master of those foxhounds near Rome about which one used to hear in peacetime has turned up in Apulia. But alas, no matter how far north our arms take us, I hardly see myself hunting in the Campagna this season.

I suppose winter is drawing round Doncaster now. It is still warm here, except at night. I am cutting down dead trees in our garden for firewood, although I have at least a faint hope that when the time comes for lighting a fire I shall no longer be there to warm my hands at it.

Your affectionate son

JOHN

1.11.43

Dearest Mamma,

This is a hurried one, as a Bag goes soon.

Mark and I meet for dinner about once or twice a week. The other night he turned up in a conveyance of gigantic size – a truck of some sort – which he parked outside our office door. When I came out the thing wouldn't start. I had to ask our driver to attend to it. Mark was mortified on behalf of the XII Lancer maintenance organisation.

I understand that Mark wants to stay on in his regiment after the War.

I don't know that I agree with Daddy if he said that there won't be agents after the war. I think there will be in some capacity, although perhaps under a different kind of principle. If agriculture is to be a British industry of any consequence after the war, it must rely on the larger units. Perhaps in years to come those units will be run on a co-operative basis. Rather an attractive thought. But you will always require somebody in the nature of the agent, even if he works under a very different economy. The point is, however, that after the war, no matter whoever or whatever one is, it will be a mistake to undertake any new function unless one is prepared to pursue it with vehemence, eagerness and curiosity and to seek specialised knowledge. There will be no 'pottering about the farms' in any profession. At least I hope not.

How I wish I had been in London when Daddy was on leave.

I hope to see Mark again tomorrow.

Best love from

JOHN

The Foreign Secretary, Mr Eden, and his party passed through Algiers on their way to the Cairo conference. By this time we had become seasoned travellers, and they had not – which, of course, was no fault of their own. But they would keep on fussing about the boxes containing their secret papers and fretting about the security arrangements, and this got on my nerves. I told them what they could do with their papers, so they decided to look after the boxes themselves and finally determined that the 'most secure' place to put the things during dinner was under the table. The boxes were put there, and we all had dinner, after which Mr Eden and his party left for the airport. I saw them off on the doorstep. When they got to the airport they discovered that they had left the boxes behind. I retrieved them from under the dinner-table and carted them out to the aerodrome, where the Secretary of State's party had been spending a cold and damp forty minutes.

The Cairo Conference between Churchill, Roosevelt and

Chiang Kai-shek was, of course, the high point in our
diplomacy that year. When it took place, in November, the
Allies were already winning the war over most of the
world. Mr Churchill and his partners had now to agree on
measures for defeating Japan.

When Mr Churchill arrived at Gibraltar in the battle-
ship *Renown*, Mr Macmillan and I flew over to meet him,
then travelled back to Algiers with him before going on to
Egypt.

In Cairo we found the security arrangements very involved. One could get into the conference area only with
great difficulty, and getting out was no easier. Mr
Churchill's house was entirely surrounded by guards.
When the Turks arrived, President Inönü turned out to be
rather deaf. He and the Prime Minister bellowed at each
other in deplorable French, so loud that the guards had to
be moved for fear that they should hear what was said.

General Chiang Kai-shek was now revealed to us in an
unexpected role, that of the big tipper. I remember the
British officer looking after him being very riled when he
was tipped a fiver. The officer came round and showed me
the fiver and asked me what he should do about it. I told
him – unless he wished to ask for more.

The conference over, we went on to Italy for an Allied
meeting at which the Russian, Vyshinsky, turned up – a
bluff man with rather nasty hard blue eyes. He had, of
course, been the prosecutor in the ghastly Moscow purge
trials. In no time at all he was asking with professional
interest what public trials of Fascists had been held in Italy.

(undated)

Dearest Mamma,

Prince Serge Obolensky, a White Russian who fought the
Bolsheviks in '17 and is now serving in Algiers as a Colonel in

the American Army, was surprised to find on his table the other
day an invitation to dine at the Soviet embassy. He accepted, and
went. He met Bogomolov (the Ambassador), Vyshinsky, and a
Russian General and Admiral. It was all very gay. They asked
him jokingly when he was coming back to Russia. They rose and
drank to the old Tsarist Guards, to the glorious Red Army and
so on; and then they drank themselves under the table (except
for Bogomolov, who has an ulcer). A crowning touch:
Obolensky says he felt very dowdy in his drab American uniform
beside the magnificent, colourful uniforms of the Soviet General
and Admiral.

Best love

JOHN

CHAPTER FOUR

Italian and Balkan Salvage Operations

AT the beginning of 1944 Mr Duff Cooper took over Mr Macmillan's representation with the French, and he and his wife, Lady Diana, arrived in Algiers. Duff Cooper had always been a *beau ideal* of mine. Brave and brilliant, the author of the celebrated biography of Talleyrand and a great friend of France, he and the lovely Lady Diana were like a breath of fresh air in Algiers with its uncomfortably humid climate and its émigré atmosphere. They behaved heroically from the start.

It would be difficult to explain to anybody who did not know that charming man how delightful and clever and many-sided he was. He was very clubbable, illuminating any gathering of men with his gay intelligence. I remember one evening after dinner when he was challenged for a bet to write a sonnet in half an hour 'On the news that Wordsworth had fathered an illegitimate son'. He did it easily. Here is the sonnet :

> Byron thou should'st be living at this hour,
> We need thy verse, thy venom and thy wit,
> To castigate the ancient hypocrite,
> We need thy pith, thy passion and thy power.
> How often did that prim old face turn sour
> Even at the mention of thy honoured name,

How oft those prudish lips have muttered 'shame'
In jealous envy of thy golden lyre,
In words worth reading had'st thou told the tale
Of what the lakeland bard was really at
When on those long excursions he set sail
For now there echoes through his tedious chat
Another voice, the third, a phantom wail
Or peevish prattle of a bastard brat.

He was chairman of White's Club at the time. So far as I know, this is the only sonnet written by a chairman of White's in half an hour.

It was hard for anybody to find a house around Algiers, and the Duff Coopers were dreadfully uncomfortable in a place with a burst boiler and a kitchen stove that had seized up. They came and had every meal in Mr Macmillan's house.

About this time Mr Churchill was lying ill in Carthage with a fever. Everybody kept on saying to him not to work and not to worry. His daughter Sarah read *Pride and Prejudice* to him from the foot of his bed. Mr Churchill commented :

What calm lives they had, those people! No worries about the French Revolution, or the crashing struggle of the Napoleonic War. Only manners controlled natural passion so far as they could, together with cultured explanations of any mischances. All this seemed to go very well with M. and B.

When he got better, Mr Churchill went to Marrakesh in Morocco to recuperate. Our telephone in Algiers was a good thermometer of the progress of the great man's return to health seven hundred miles away. Mr Macmillan, after listening for several days to Mr Churchill's voice booming over the telephone, flew to Marrakesh to visit him. I was left with the Duff Coopers in Algiers.

Early that year, Diana Cooper wrote to a friend in England. 'Harold Macmillan,' she said, 'is our saviour. He's a splendid man. He feeds us and warms us and washes us. One day he'll be Prime Minister. I've put my money (nay, my shirt) on him. He's my horse.' Twenty-five years later, when Diana's horse had romped home to become Prime Minister, she used to call him 'my horse' – which sometimes led to mystification. I remember her asking me at a luncheon party, 'What is my horse doing today?' I said, 'Well at this actual moment, your horse is giving luncheon to the King of Nepal.' *Stupeur dans l'assistance*. Neither of us bothered to explain.

11.1.44

Dearest Mamma,

The last event on the French side before we ceased to be associated with it was the reception in Algiers, by the National Committee, of President Beneš. They made a great fuss of him. I went out to the airfield to represent Uncle Harold at his arrival. It was a filthy afternoon, pouring with rain. Waiting at the end of the runway I found a band and standard and guard of honour of 200 Negro troops, shivering and soaked. A crowd of miserable '*hautes personnalités civiles et militaires*' headed by Charlie de Gaulle himself, waited and waited in the downpour. The Baron d'Huart of the Protocol Division of the French Commissariat for Foreign Affairs, who had come without a mackintosh, hurried about, marshalling us, without a stitch of dry clothing on him. We waited for three hours. At last an aircraft appeared. A flutter of relief passed through the reception committee, the guard of honour stiffened, the band shook the rain out of their instruments. The aircraft taxied up to us and stopped. The Baron d'Huart hurried forward. I asked Massigli's secretary in a last minute whisper whether it would be all right

H

if I spoke to the President in English. The door of the aeroplane was opened. And out stepped an individual with a *café-au-lait* complexion. Everybody gasped. The Baron, with his eyes popping out of his head, enquired of the arrival who he was. He was the newly appointed Minister from Cuba, and delighted with his reception.

Beneš arrived an hour later, and in the dark, having been delayed by bad weather.

The Baron rose from his influenza bed yesterday.

Best love from

JOHN

After that I had to do a lot of flying about. I flew to Italy in the aeroplane of the Commander-in-Chief, General Wilson, with his military assistant, Colonel Mark Chapman-Walker, to set up yet another office for Mr Macmillan. This I succeeded in doing in the Palace of Caserta, where General Alexander had his headquarters. I got hold of some rooms on the north side of the Palace and scrounged some furniture, and was rather pleased with what I had done in competition with the headquarters staff who were all after the same thing. It is no joke reserving accommodation for other people. These apartments, facing north, were frightfully cold in winter. An icy wind blew down from the Apennines. When Mr Macmillan's staff arrived, and we all sat shivering at work in our overcoats, hard looks were directed towards me. The wind whistled through the chinks in the huge and ancient windows. Various generals on the *south* side basked in the beams of a sun which, although wintry, took the chill out of their bones. There was nothing to do about it except bide one's time and wait for the summer, when the generals on the south side were pouring with sweat at their desks and lashing their military assistants for lack of foresight, while we on the north side were comparatively cool. All was then forgiven.

Caserta, the great country palace of the Kings of Naples, has some fine baroque rooms and a magnificent grand staircase. It is enormous, on a Versailles scale – and like Versailles the proportion of inglorious draughty corridors and chilly attics greatly exceeds that of the grand salons. Sitting there, we could not but admire Louis XIV for the racket that he worked in getting his aristocracy to endure the frozen and cramped horrors of their court life at Versailles while despising them for putting up with it.

Jeeps and other military vehicles rattled in and out of the courtyards. A soldier had stuffed a bag of peanuts into the mouth of one of the stone lions that guard the great stairs. In a vast white and gold chamber, army administrative officers grappled with their papers at barrack-room tables, while from a cloud in the middle of the painted ceiling a figure like God, looking pretty fed up, glared down at the scene.

I took over a cottage just outside the park as sleeping quarters for the members of Mr Macmillan's chancery and a house in Naples for Mr Macmillan.

Then back we went to Algiers; and on to Marrakesh to see Mr Churchill. Mr Macmillan read *Emma* on the way. We reached Marrakesh at 10.30 p.m. and went to Mr Churchill's villa, where we found them all still at dinner — Mr. Churchill, Mrs Churchill, their daughter Sarah, Lord Beaverbrook, the Duff Coopers and the members of the Prime Minister's private office.

Mr Churchill was in great form. They were talking about Italy. What about the King of Italy and his Prime Minister, Marshal Badoglio? The Prime Minister was all for keeping them on at present. 'When I want to lift a pot of hot coffee', he said, 'I prefer to keep the handle.' After which, zestfully but quietly, Mr Churchill started singing some old-time music-hall songs, talking the while to Lady Diana Cooper, beating time with a fork, and punctuating his songs with remarks like 'And now do you remember this one, Diana?' I loved it all, but I noticed that Lord Beaverbrook looked bored. Perhaps he didn't care for small talk. Yet he was very courteous to me in a friendly but distant way.

We next went to London for another round of consultations, then returned to Italy. Visiting the headquarters of the Eighth Army, now commanded by General Oliver Leese, we found them in an olive grove, just a few tents and caravans. The band of a Guards regiment happened to be on hand, and the General summoned them to play in Mr Macmillan's honour. They played nice old Hyde Park bandstand tunes – novel echoes in an Arcadian valley of the Apennines. The man with the cymbals was six feet six inches tall, and the other bandsmen called him 'Clap-hands Charlie'.

Mr Macmillan was now exceedingly busy with Harold Caccia, notably on the policies to be applied once Rome was liberated. But he was handicapped during this visit by not having his usual communications with London – he did not have his own cyphers with him. He had to use army channels, which restricted the candour expected of him by the Prime Minister, to whom he reported.

I do not mean that Mr Macmillan was given to saying one thing to the admirals, generals and air marshals to their faces and another thing behind their backs to the Prime Minister; but confidential reports of the kind that he had to render ought to be rendered in confidence. This applies in all the higher walks of life – in business, in politics, but particularly in diplomacy. That you do not wish other people to know what you have said about them in the course of duty does not imply bad faith; it simply implies candour in proper reporting without unduly gumming up the works. I made a note that we should never be without our own cyphers and cypher clerks.

We spent a night in the Parco Hotel at Naples, which had been taken over by the army and was rather over-crowded. Mr Macmillan and I had to share a room, and he recorded in his diary: 'John shares a room with me. He is a restless moaning sleeper.' Time and again my wife has confirmed this.

31.3.44

Dearest Mamma,

The evening before I left Italy I motored round the Bay of Naples in search of Andrew [Duke of Devonshire] whose battalion were resting in the district. I found him, after quite a hunt, near Sorrento, and dined with him and Tom Egerton in the latter's company mess. I also saw Simon Phipps, whom I've always liked. They had good billets and had managed to make themselves very comfortable. They had been in a cold and wet part of the line.

Returning to Naples after dinner I rounded a bend on a sort of corniche road and a great glare in the sky above Vesuvius was revealed, reflected by a scarlet path across the sea in the bay. And so Vesuvius was erupting. Two streams of lava were running down the mountainside. From the distance where I was they appeared only as scarlet threads; but the smoke and ashes clouded the light of the head-lamps like fog.

Next morning we went to Cairo by aeroplane with General Wilson. A long and tedious journey, which the old General beguiled with *Sixty-three Years*, an autobiography by the Earl of Onslow (coronet on the dust-jacket) and a whodunit by Ellery Queen. We landed for half an hour at Malta, where Lord Gort turned up to say hello to the General and my master, and reached Cairo in time for dinner. We stayed at the Caseys' old house (property of Mr Chester Beatty) near the Pyramids. Lord Moyne now uses it as a guest-house and week-end villa. He doesn't utter much on any score; but, my goodness, his face is a chapter in itself on more than one subject!

The only remark of Lord Moyne's that I recall was made when the local admiral (whose name I forget) whose undoubted charm is said to lie partly in his adventurous mind, launched forth at luncheon on speculations as to the ultimate purpose of human nature. Lord Moyne, who had been quite silent, sat up and muttered, 'The purpose of human nature, indeed of all nature, is to propagate its species.' Upon which he blinked and relapsed into silence again.

My last evening in Cairo, Lady Smart, the wife of the Oriental Secretary at the Embassy, told me she had Dick Wyndham staying with her. I wonder what he's up to there? As I flew away at half past twelve that night, I never saw him.

Then we spent one night in Algiers and passed on to Naples again. The eruption had expended itself. I suppose you have read of it in the papers and how it is the worst for whatnot number of years. Vesuvius lay under a cloak of its own ash and looked like a giant slag-heap. It was an interesting sight from the air : one saw the solidified tongues of lava protruding into the plain, having engulfed villages.

Then we came back to Algiers for four days. We return to Italy again tomorrow, leaving at 7 a.m., so it's time this letter stopped.

It is not for the private secretary to ask whether all these journeys are really necessary. Nor are they the fault of the master. As the Irish Member of Parliament said, 'I am not a bird; I cannot be in two places at once.' But in a theatre of operations which covers almost the whole of the ancient world to be so would be the only happier solution.

Best love from

JOHN

Dearest Mamma,

This letter comes to you from a *wagon-lit* in an Italian railway siding. It is rather agreeable being in one again. The little notices such as '*En Cas de Danger Tirer l'Anneau*' ring the bell for memories of one or two trips before the war.

Lord Gort came to stay with us in Algiers before we left for here. It was purely a private visit, but when the French got wind of it they decided to give him an official welcome. I sallied out to meet him at the airfield. There I found a battalion of soldiers, a band and colours, and a reception committee headed by an old geyser called de Witasse who is Chef de Protocol at the Commissariat of Foreign Affairs. Lord Gort duly arrived, and was done the honours; and next day the local paper *Alger Républicain*, never very skilful at avoiding misprints, in reporting the scene came out with a stunner: '*La musique de l'Aviation Française a rendu "God shave the King"*.'

Best love from

JOHN

On these journeys Mr Macmillan read Dickens and then embarked on Boswell's *Life of Johnson*. I ploughed my way through Gibbon. We exchanged comments about these various works, Mr Macmillan observing that *David Copperfield* was a noble and wonderful book, his favourite Dickens, and that Boswell was just the thing for air travel.

Mr Macmillan talked about the Russians, Vyshinsky and Bogomolov. Vyshinsky had charm, he thought, which Bogomolov had not. Bogomolov was naturally shifty; Vyshinsky was naturally frank. Vyshinsky would laugh with you and stand you a good dinner and drink vodka with you – and then arrange for you to be quietly shot through the back of the head. Bogomolov would entertain you to a serious and rather dreary repast where you would be slowly poisoned in indifferent French wine, after which you would slowly die.

To me, however, Bogomolov had one endearing trait. His favourite book was *Three Men in a Boat*, and he and his wife used to quote passages to each other from memory and in Russian and then roar with laughter, sometimes causing mystification to others present. On one of these occasions I asked Bogomolov: 'Are you laughing at *us*?' He said, no, he was laughing at *Trois hommes dans un bateau* I was puzzled until I realised that it was a case of two Russians and three men and a boat.

Well, Mr Macmillan and I had Dickens and Boswell and Gibbon, and the Bogomolovs had *Three Men in a Boat*. I think that our reading did us all credit.

The King came to visit Italy.

4.8.44

Dearest Mamma,

I haven't written for a long time, and I am so sorry. I've been disorganised with things to do.

A regulation, at which I am not qualified to cavil, forbids me to say where we are now. Sir Alan Lascelles, of course, knows. Letters should be addressed to the Office of the Resident Minister, Mediterranean, and marked 'Naples Bag'.

The King's visit seems to have been a success, and the monarch himself to have enjoyed it. His staff, however, were hampered by upset insides (a trouble which besets many of our unacclimatised visitors) and Sir Piers Legh went about looking very uncomfortable.

The whole programme was well arranged, from the initial luncheon party, for 80, in one of the great baroque salons of the Palace of Caserta (a setting finer than that which any of the guest of honour's own houses could boast) to the *al fresco* meal in the country at the end, after a parade of troops, when General Jumbo Wilson's chair collapsed beneath him, and the royal sense of humour came creaking into action.

Alas, none of us can occupy Uncle Archie's [Lord Rosebery's] house, as the Italian government came and asked Sir Noel Charles [Ambassador to Italy] if they might use it, and Charles went and said yes. By the time the news reached us it was too late to tell him to get it back.

Best love from

JOHN

In the meantime the Warsaw rising had begun, U.S. troops had broken through at Avranches in France, a German army had been exterminated in the Falaise Gap, the Eighth Army had taken Florence. There was a great Russian offensive in Bessarabia and Roumania, and General de Gaulle had entered Paris in the wake of the Allied troops and established his provisional government. The armies in Italy had been depleted by the withdrawal of soldiers to land on the French Riviera. At the same time, a nasty and unexpected sideshow was developing in Greece. Before long, we knew that it was more than a sideshow. But for the present I was laid up.

September 1944

Dearest Mamma,

I am now in the local military hospital with jaundice. It is a very good hospital, with charming nursing sisters who have come here via Cairo, the Western Desert and French North Africa. There are only eight officers in my ward, which has beds for sixteen. And by a happy coincidence my companions don't like the wireless very much, so by common consent we generally only turn it on for the news.

I spend my time reading, sleeping or contemplating my honey-coloured toes, which frequently confront me by sticking out of the end of the bed. They are such an odd colour that, like the man who in the middle of the night mistook one of his for an intruder's hand and shot it off, I at first was hardly willing to believe that they were part of me.

This morning I read old Gosse's book *Father and Son*. What an ass Gosse *père* must have been! When the onion-vendor came round singing :

> 'Here's your rope
> To hang the Pope'

– the old fool ran out of the house and quite seriously gave the man a penny to reward 'his Godly attitude towards the Papacy'. Shades of Mr Knox.

I also have that arid economic work *The Middle Way* by H. Macmillan, the quite unnecessary dullness of which is enough to turn anybody yellow who isn't so already.

Young Michael Spears (son of Sir Edward) has turned up in our office to lend a hand at the Greek desk. I like him, although he seldom speaks. He is a clever chap. He was at Eton with me, but was hardly a crony of mine there – for one thing he was away a great deal of the time being ill. He has been employed lately as a temporary member of the Foreign Service in our Embassy to the Greeks. Having come here by sea he was able to bring a box-full of books, many of which are under my hospital bed at the moment.

You say hurry up and get married. All right, I'll start looking round among the Neapolitans as soon as I get up. Of course they are all Roman Catholics.

I should imagine that dignity is not the forte of the Roman aristocracy. Otherwise they would not have been in such a hurry after the liberation of Rome to recount with much self-pity the hardships they had suffered during the German occupation. Those who (very properly, I think) stopped them short with the observation that they had only themselves to thank for the mess they had got into were apt to be met by a shocked silence such as an astounding breach of bad taste might cause.

Could their attitude, even if unconscious, be that aristocracy knows no frontiers, that while political policy from time to time requires that they should cut themselves off by war from the upper class in other countries, we are nevertheless all members alike of the good old club, the Noble Society for Keeping the Plebs in Its Place?

They have quite an armoury of charm and beauty – dashing weapons, but not likely to be very effective in the difficulties which lie ahead of them in Italy after the Allies have gone.

However, who am I to talk? I've never met any of them.

A South African A.T.S. officer was brought to dinner with us before I came to hospital. After dinner she said to me: 'Where does one go to speak to the fairies?' Bored, I replied: 'To the bottom of the garden, I suppose.'

She commented rather acidly that she would have thought we'd have had better facilities than *that*.

So then I realised that the silly woman wished to go to the lavatory. What odd phrases people resort to.

Best love from

JOHN

October 2nd, 1944

Dearest Mamma,

I hope to be out of hospital in a day or two.

This morning I got up and went for a walk. I pottered down the road towards A.F.H.Q., where, outside our office, I came across a large Rolls Royce with Lady Charles, reading a book, inside. Upon my bidding her good morning she flicked back the pages of the book to reveal a book-plate consisting of an imposing coat of arms and – the name of the Duchess of Sermonetta!* She proclaimed herself a firm believer in the Duchess who, she said, had a good record and had been obliged to go into hiding at one time before Rome was liberated. There (according to Lady C) among other, more serious privations, she felt much the lack of facilities for indulging her pleasure in cards. So she taught her faithful maid, Gertie, to play pinochle, which, however, Gertie never learnt to play anything but badly. Thus they would beguile the lonely hours, the Duchess exasperated by

---

* An acquaintance of my mother.

Gertie's slowness. 'Oh *Gertie*! Do hurry up!' 'If your Grace hurries me, I shall refuse to play.'

I can only imagine one worse fate for Gertie, and that would consist of being shut up with you, dear Mamma, and being taught to play bezique.

Best love from

JOHN

October 15th, 1944

Dearest Mamma,

This one comes from a Rome airfield where I am waiting to get on an aeroplane going to Caserta, having spent a few days up here after coming out of hospital.

My first evening in Rome I dined with Dan Ranfurly who took me to a party in the house of some Romans called di Leonardi. This sort of Italian is now in an extraordinary situation; they have butlers and footmen, but not enough food; large apartments or houses, but seldom electric light and never hot water or fuel for the central heating. They still maintain some luxury, but have lost all means of comfort. There were lots of pretty girls. I do not remember the names of any of them except one, the daughter of Varé of *Laughing Diplomat* and *Heavenly Trousers* fame.

I stayed first with Harold Caccia, and then, when he departed on a trip to the north, Lady Charles asked me to the Embassy, which was very enjoyable.

Count John de Salis wished to be remembered to Daddy, in whose squadron he used to be. I doubt whether he was the latter's cup of tea, but he was very kind to me, lending me his car and asking me to lunch. He is now a colonel in the uniform of the Irish Guards and liaises between the local Military and the Vatican authorities, and is exploited by many others as a benevolent bottle-washer. When I lunched with him I met his staff-captain, Uttley, who used to be tutor to the Duchess of Sermonetta's son, and Donna Orieta Doria, daughter of Prince

Doria.* After lunch we all went up to Villa Doria Pamphili, unkempt – the Dorias had to make themselves scarce for part of the war because they were notorious for their anti-Fascist and pro-British sentiments – but still enchanting. The Germans had occupied the house, had practised revolver shots at the figures on the exterior, had painted crude frescoes indoors depicting Marxists, Jews and democrats enslaving the common people, had stolen all the furniture and, when they left, had planted mines in the grounds.

Lady Charles sent me, rather unwilling, to call on your Duchess of Sermonetta; but I enjoyed the visit. The old girl was in bed, having contracted a chill at the funeral of a dear friend who, so far as I could gather, had met her death by falling down a manhole in her own garden. I was piloted to the bedroom by the terrifying Gertie (allergic to cards). The Duchess much the *grande dame*, suited by her surroundings (Palazzo Caetani in the shell of a coliseum) but very lively. She was full of anecdotes of England and Italy, and would not let me leave until Gertie eventually appeared on the scene with a new visitor, Princess Colonna.

Sir D'Arcy Osborne, generating an atmosphere of courtly charm about himself, turned up at the Embassy yesterday afternoon to take Sir Noel Charles golfing. He is at last moving out of the Vatican into a house in Rome.

An American Negro clergyman who is travelling my way says the aeroplane has at last turned up; so I will now close.

With best love from

JOHN

At the beginning of November 1944 I accompanied Mr Macmillan to Athens to stay with the Ambassador, Mr Leeper. The Greeks were having a tough time with very little food, a runaway inflation and a revolution in the offing. What with the British Cabinet Minister, Mr

* Mayor of Rome, who married the Englishwoman who had nursed him in the 1914–18 war.

Macmillan, and the British Ambassador, surrounded by pundits sent out from the British Treasury, and several other experts on supply, a lot of doctors were gathered round the patient, whose illness was marked by ceaseless chatter and much political slogan-writing on walls. Greece was in a mess, and the countryside around Athens was largely controlled by Greek Communist guerrillas. They waved in a friendly way when I went by, though one of them nearly killed me later on.

In the meanwhile changes had been taking place in Italy, which had been dominated by an Allied Control Commission in Rome. It was agreed that the Italians had worked their passage on the Allied side long enough for the word 'Control' to be dropped from the title. Mr Macmillan was made Acting President of the Allied Commission, and this meant setting up yet another branch office – in Rome – for what I had come to call the firm of Macmillan's Mediterranean and Balkan Salvage Enterprise.

It was decided that Mr Macmillan should go to London and then to Washington to discuss future political and administrative arrangements for Italy, and we set off by air from Caserta at 8 a.m. on 22 November 1944. We landed at Marseilles, where the captain asked for petrol and the way. After two hours' delay we set off again in bad weather only to land at Dijon, where the captain decided to give up. We pushed on by car in pouring rain, reached Paris in the early hours of the morning, and sought accommodation in the Hotel Raphael. Mr Macmillan took advantage of this enforced delay to complete a long paper embodying all his recommendations for Italian reform.

Arrived in London, we established ourselves in the Cabinet Offices. There followed meetings with people from the Foreign Office and the War Office. Mr Macmillan said that he wanted to avoid Ministers – and especially the Prime Minister – until he had cleared his proposals at the departmental level, and this he managed to do. But it was a funny sort of set-up – Macmillan and his young private secretary on the one side and all the resources of great Departments of State on the other.

Mr Macmillan then went to dine at 10 Downing Street and a day or two later a more confident Mr Macmillan did business at the American Embassy. His paper for the War Cabinet was now in draft. He saw the Prime Minister again, then Mr Eden, and afterwards attended a meeting of Ministers at No. 10.

By now the expected revolution had broken out in Greece, but Italy was still without a Government, and we worked away in the Cabinet Offices on our Italian business. This was a period when the Prime Minister was quite overloaded with work. Although Mr Macmillan had seen him more than once, and had indeed dined with him, it may have temporarily escaped Mr Churchill's mind that Mr Macmillan was also responsible for Greece. It may even, such were Mr Churchill's preoccupations, have escaped him, except when he was actually seeing Mr Macmillan, that the latter was in England. Thus at Question Time in the House of Commons on 5 December Mr Churchill spoke to the effect that the situation in Greece was in capable hands, including those of his Right Honourable Friend the Member for Stockton-on-Tees – Mr Macmillan. At this Mr Shinwell rose and, pointing across the chamber, observed that Mr Macmillan was sitting on the benches opposite – as if to say, 'Look, he's not in Athens at all!' The Prime Minister recovered himself and his memory and said, 'I was speaking of the general principle, and not with reference to the exact location of the Right Honourable

Gentleman.' But he looked annoyed, and I thought that we might be in for trouble – as we were.

It seemed likely that Communist extremists would try to seize the city of Athens, and this they soon attempted in an effort to crush all forms of Greek expression but their own. But we were not going to stand aside, any more than we had stood aside in 1941. In the House on 8 December Mr Churchill declared that we were ready to risk our blood and such treasure as we had to defend Athens and our honour. Mr Eden, winding up the debate, described our purpose as helping Democracy once again to play a part in the land of its birth. Immediately afterwards, the Prime Minister sent for Mr Macmillan – and made a sudden attack on him. He all but accused him of having deserted his post, despite the fact that Mr Macmillan had come to England on Churchill's own orders. Mr Macmillan pointed out that only a few hours previously the Prime Minister had sent a telegram to the President saying that Macmillan would be in Washington in a day or two to discuss all Italian affairs and supply for the Mediterranean area and indeed for liberated Europe generally. Mr Churchill had to give way, but still said that he felt instinctively that Mr Macmillan should return to his post. Back we went to the Mediterranean, which is what I think Mr Macmillan anyhow wanted to do. Others were fagged to see to his business in Washington.

On arriving at an airfield outside Athens there was an hour's delay because the road into the city was under shellfire from the insurgents. Armoured cars were summoned to take us to the British Embassy, where we found ourselves besieged and under fire, the rebels holding four-fifths of Athens and the Piraeus and all the hills around. The entire Embassy staff had moved into the Embassy together with a military guard. We were very crowded, and I slept on a sofa in the Chancery. We mostly used kerosene lamps, but an electric generator was brought into use when better lighting was really essential. If you have to be caught in a battle, I reflected, the last place to be is in a house designed for civilised life with the water cut off and vastly more occupants than it was ever meant to contain. With both sexes involved, it was all the harder to preserve the graces, though everybody managed quite cheerfully. But for future battles I should much prefer the open air.

On walking into the Embassy I met for the first time the delightful Osbert Lancaster, who was in charge of press relations and discharged his duties, as I quickly discovered, with tact, wit, wisdom and charm. With fanatical Greeks on rooftops taking pot-shots at one wherever one went, not to speak of a rebel battery lobbing shells on us from outside the city, Osbert had quite a job keeping in touch with his flock, the press, and keeping them in touch with the truth. But, being Osbert, he managed.

Harold Caccia had become Mr Macmillan's personal representative in Athens, and he zoomed around fearlessly in a jeep until it was destroyed by a shell. Happily Harold was not in it at the time, but alas, his American driver, Tchaikovsky, was killed. Previously the charming Tchaikovsky had been Harold Caccia's devoted driver in Rome, and we were all very sad at his death.

As the odd house-party in the Embassy went on, I soon realised that one bore about being besieged if you are a young man is the lack of opportunities for exercise. One afternoon I came across a piece of rope and decided to go skipping in the small Embassy garden. I hadn't been skipping very long when ping, a bullet landed at my feet. I looked up, and there was a man on a neighbouring rooftop

I

aiming a rifle at me. He kept on taking pot-shots at me while I darted about trying to avoid them. Osbert Lancaster appeared at the french windows and called out: 'What *are* you doing?' I explained that a man up there was trying to kill me.

Osbert said: 'Hang on!' and disappeared. Presently he reappeared at the french windows, shouting, 'Keep him in play; we have summoned the military to come and pick him off.' By this time I was getting rather fed up. The Ambassador, the Ambassadress, Mr Macmillan and various members of the Embassy staff now appeared at the window, shouting, 'Keep it up, keep it up.' This I did. At one stage I dived into the border, only to hear the Ambassadress cry from behind the french window: 'Oh, John, not the dahlias!' So I dashed for shelter into the potting-shed, from time to time poking my head out of the door (ping, ping, came the bullets) and calling to my friends to ask how long this lark was likely to last. They said not to despair. An armoured car lumbered up and the man was picked off. Osbert said: 'That chap made you skip, didn't he?' We then got on with our work.

I flew about quite a lot, and once, arriving at a Greek airfield and finding nobody to meet me, I asked if it was possible to telephone the British Embassy. The answer was yes – through an exchange held by the insurgents. 'But they are always very good to us; they always put us through!' It might have been Ireland in the Troubles.

The rebels held the perimeter of the city, and we had the middle. Thus we were beleaguered, but as we had armoured cars and they had not, the blockade could be run in safety. Otherwise, it was prudent to remain indoors, as I had learnt from my skipping experience. We lived on hard rations and some of us enjoyed a Greek drink, ouzo, which was brought in at night by a capable Greek ouzo-runner.

December 18, 1944

Dearest Mamma,

There are fifty persons living huggermugger in the Embassy. I sleep on a sofa in the chancery. There is plenty to eat of the bully-beef-and-biscuits type. The electric light and water in the city have been cut off. We are fortunate in having an auxiliary electricity generator, and a water well in the garden from which water is carried to the house in buckets. We have a small guard of soldiers under the command of a Major of the 10th called Vere Barker.

When, the day before yesterday, I flew back to Caserta for a night on business, the pilot lost his way. On the return journey to Greece (in another aircraft) I asked the pilot if he knew the way; he said he did, and, upon my travelling companion, a Brigadier Mainwaring, asking where he was going, he replied with the name of an airfield in rebel hands. I count myself lucky to be here.

We work here with difficulties on either side : on the one hand the extremists among the rebels, who precipitated the conflict because they had little hope of achieving by constitutional means through the ballot-box those aims which they are now pursuing with bullets; on the other, those supporters of the Government who would carry on the fight, not simply to restore peace, but until their opponents have been eliminated. So in both camps there are persons who are not in a hurry to end the fight. The Archbishop's a good chap : His Beatitude.

I am glad our journey was switched to here as Athens is obviously more fun to be in now than Washington. Perhaps I may pay you another visit after Christmas.

With best love

JOHN

On the night of 12 December a heavy attack was made on the Embassy. It was repelled by the military. While it is never funny to be attacked, it is doubly tiresome if you happen to be a male civilian. You just have to sit there doing nothing. I read one of my volumes of Gibbon which I was carrying about at the time. It was bound in blue cloth, and after the attack had been repulsed and we were sitting down to our bully-beef-and-biscuits I found that I had sweated so much that the blue had come off on the palms of my hands.

As the siege went on, we could do little more than take military measures to break it while planning for the political future of Greece. The Embassy was by now midway between the perimeter of the British-held city centre and the Communist lines – in other words, in no man's land. We had been making wry jokes about the possibility of being overrun. I used to wake up on the Chancery sofa in the morning, go to my desk and get on with my work, which consisted chiefly of drafting telegrams and despatches for the consideration of various grandees in London. I was told that it was the duty of His Majesty's Foreign Service to prepare as best they could for any eventuality, but with due regard to precedent. Thus in the course of the attack on the night of 12 December, becoming bored with Gibbon, I did a draft despatch to the Foreign Secretary about outstanding business. I ended by saying that the enemy were at the gates (which they were) and that

therefore soon, Sir,
　　I may cease to have the honour to be
　　　　Your obedient servant . . .

But the enemy were driven away, and the next thing was to organise the final clearing of Athens and chase the insurgents into open country.

Then at Christmas there was a remarkable development. The Ambassadress, who was of a High Church turn of mind, arranged a midnight mass in the drawing-room of our crowded Embassy on Christmas Eve. The clergyman who was to conduct the mass arrived in an armoured car and preached what Osbert Lancaster described as a seasonable and apposite sermon, referring to the Herald Angels as 'God's airborne division'. Before the service was over there was a knock at the door, which I happened to be sitting by. I opened it, to be told that an important telegram had arrived, whereupon I extracted one of the cypher clerks from the congregation and we went off to decypher the telegram. By 1 a.m. we were able to produce the startling news that the Prime Minister was arriving next day, and I remember rounding off the opening hours of Christmas morning before going to sleep by singing 'Christians seek not yet repose' in the Chancery.

We had very little repose during the next day or two, but the Prime Minister's visit set the Greeks upon a course which Mr Macmillan had been advocating. Mr Churchill's presence cleared the air, which was becoming thick with telegrams.

It was a bitterly cold morning when he landed at Kalamaki airfield, which for the occasion was heavily guarded. Those of us who stood shivering on the tarmac were looking forward to getting back indoors. Mr Churchill, in his Air Commodore's uniform, appeared at the door of his aeroplane and beckoned the senior people up the steps. He sniffed the sharp air and said : 'Very chilly, isn't it ? A glass of brandy, I think.' Very sensibly, they all retired into the aircraft, while the rest of us waited outside, half frozen.

It was not thought safe for the Prime Minister and his party to spend much time in Athens. Escorted by several

armoured cars, Mr Churchill was taken to the security of
H.M.S. *Ajax*, anchored off Piraeus. Because it was Christmas Day, some of the sailors had got themselves up in
fancy dress, for their own amusement. When the Regent of
Greece, the richly robed Archbishop Damaskinos, arrived
to see the Prime Minister, the sailors took him for part of
their own show and danced around him. We had some
difficulty in explaining this to the Archbishop.

On Boxing Day Mr Churchill visited the Embassy in an
armoured car with a military escort. Jock Colville, his
private secretary, got a raspberry from him for not bringing a revolver, though I noticed that the Prime Minister
had one. Jock in the meantime had scrounged a tommy-gun.
Mr Churchill found time to address the Embassy staff, and
we were all much moved – except possibly the American
Minister, who had been invited in as a courtesy and had to
listen to some strong strictures on U.S. policy towards
Greece.

That night, without benefit of electric light, there was a
conference in the Greek Foreign Office. All the swells were
present. They used hurricane lamps, there was no heat, and
everybody wore overcoats. I can still see them huddled
round the table in that bleak room, their faces only dimly
lit. The Archbishop's torso was crowned by his tall
archiepiscopal hat, sticking up in the flickering light like a
thin mountain peak; the hurricane lamps illuminated his
body and the lower part of his face, but his head and
his hat were only half seen in the gloom. Field-Marshal
Alexander was there, immaculate and impassive, with Mr
Eden, the American Minister, the French Minister and the
Soviet Military Representative.

I remember the Archbishop-Regent at one point eulogis-
ing certain Greek political figures, when Mr Macmillan

remarked, with a deprecating smile, that one might almost think that His Beatitude had been preparing a chit for St Peter in order to get these gentlemen into Heaven. Oh no, replied the prelate; he was simply trying to be helpful in a difficult situation – and it was the earth that they were after.

Returning to Rome soon after Christmas 1944, I set up an office for Mr Macmillan in the former Fascist Ministry of Corporations, while he had a house in the Via Nomentana, just beyond Mussolini's late official residence, the Villa Torlonia. I was told that his house had belonged to an ex-Commissioner of Works. It was done up in a terrible neo-Baroque style like a luxurious brothel, but it suited us all right, and I believe that the characters of Mr Macmillan and his staff enabled us all to bear the odium with aplomb.

December 31st, 1944

Dearest Mamma,

Thank you for all the nice things you say about the medal in your letter. I stupidly forgot to tell you about it when I was in London.

By a coincidence I am writing this letter at midnight. In half an hour's time it will be exactly two years ago to the minute that I took off in an aeroplane from Cornwall for foreign parts. Since then few persons of my age can have had such an interesting time – or, for that matter, a better master.

Bless you,
Best love from

JOHN

Mr Macmillan arrived next day from Athens via Caserta, none the worse for his continual travelling around the turbulent territory over which he presided politically. When I met him he was terribly tired, but in spirit as alive and alert and chipper as always.

Then one day when I was on a visit to our office in the
Palace of Caserta near Naples, the news came through of
the surrender of the German forces in Italy. We went down
to the office of our American colleagues on the floor
below, where they had a wireless, to listen to the announcement. Mr Offie, the American in charge, was keen to
make it a happy surprise for the junior members of his
staff, but wondered how to get them into the room to listen
to the wireless beforehand? Resourcefully, he told them
that Lady Dorothy Macmillan was a considerable author
of hymns, and that they must all come along as a courtesy
to Mr Macmillan to hear one of them broadcast.

After the end of the war in Europe and the break-up of
the Coalition Government in Britain, Mr Macmillan
returned to London to become Secretary of State for Air in
Mr Churchill's Caretaker Government. I went with him to
the Air Ministry.

On the fall of the Caretaker Government in 1945 I was
transferred to Washington to be Private Secretary to Mr
R. H. Brand, head of the British Treasury Delegation and
Chairman of the British Supply Council in North America,
to which I also became Assistant Secretary. The Ambassador in Washington was Lord Halifax. We were soon
immersed in the negotiations for the famous – or as Lord
Beaverbrook would have called it, the infamous – American
loan of a thousand million dollars to bolster up the British
economy. Lord Keynes came out as the principal negotiator
from Britain, and the loan was eventually agreed.

Washington was very overcrowded, and it was only
with difficulty that I secured an attic room in a hotel of
sorts, overlooking the premises of a newspaper with a
night-long clatter of printing presses. But it served as a
base from which to look around, and presently I ran into an

American friend, Kenneth Pendar, who had been one of Robert Murphy's agents in North Africa. We set ourselves up together in a house in Georgetown.

November 25th 1945

Dearest Mamma,

My friend Pendar and I are now established in a very nice house in Georgetown. The owner is in the Balkans. May she stay there : we are doing our best to keep her there; we have just got her introduced to the King of Roumania. We have a coloured servant called Hattie, who, in common with the late Lord Kitchener, is allergic to cats, but that is her affair, especially as we don't keep a cat. The nucleus of our *lares* and *penates* is a valuable silver mug called Cornelius Vanderbilt : that name is engraved in large letters upon it. The mug's presence is inexplicable, but it and the name have a salutary effect upon the tradesmen so far as credit is concerned, although I rather think they cause a rise in prices.

I went to lunch with the Halifaxes. Lord Halifax recalled his Eton days with my father, who, he said, was an erratic and irresponsible football player. So was I. I was all but the other side's secret weapon. Lord Keynes, in knowledge, capacity and activity, of course, dominates the scene in the current interminable negotiations. But Lord Halifax's interventions, well-spaced, well-timed, and presented with simplicity, dignity and honesty, have great effect. Lord Keynes gallops his mind at all the problems, threading his way at speed among them, like a superlative rider with a superlative horse in a bending race. He sports with the great intricacies. Others may envy his brilliant feats, but cannot emulate them : they can only watch and comment from the stands. And that is where Lord Halifax comes in. Standing among the crowd he can often strike a common note; while Lord Keynes, the genius, for all his charm, performs alone.

with best love from

JOHN

After the loan negotiations had been completed I returned to England with the head of my delegation, by now Lord Brand. The Treasury offered me further adventures abroad, this time in Egypt, but I decided to retire. I was all of twenty-five.

CHAPTER FIVE

New Brooms
in Old Queen Street

AFTER my retirement from the Civil Service I spent
the best part of a sabbatical year, then became bored
and went and joined the Conservative Research Department.

In the meantime I had made a journey with Mr Macmillan to Persia and India. We flew to Abadan, toured the
oilfields, went up to Teheran, hitch-hiked to Bombay on a
tanker. We visited Calcutta, Delhi, the Central Provinces
and Karachi. In Delhi the Viceroy, Lord Wavell, said that
given the troops he could hold India; but would the British
public or the troops stand for it? In Karachi Mr Jinnah said
that if there was partition, there would be a blood-bath. He
was proved right.

Returning to London on a cold February day in 1947 I
found a message from Lord Cranborne inviting me for the
weekend at Hatfield. Thither I went. Lady Cranborne is
one of my Wyndham-Quin cousins. On walking into the
drawing-room I found a beautiful girl whom I had never
met before, and who turned out to be her sister. I decided
there and then to marry this girl, and I did so.

I found the Conservative Research Department a fascinating place. It was a self-contained section of the Conservative Party headquarters, separately housed at 24 Old

Queen Street. It had been founded in 1929 by Mr Baldwin, rather half-heartedly and on the understanding that it would be taken over by Neville Chamberlain, which it was. Mr Chamberlain wanted a group of men who would devil for him, and work out the application of measures which would be given them as the party's policy. This at the time meant mainly an elaboration of a protective tariff. Others had a more academic conception of a group ranging at large over the whole field of unsolved problems and suggesting conclusions from which party policy might be constructed. Perhaps this latter attitude was too academic at a time when the need was for an immediate programme to restore the damaged morale of the party, then struggling to recover from the blunder of 'safety first'.

At all events the department was duly set up, as a body independent of the Conservative Central Office, by a minute of the Leader, who appointed Mr Chamberlain as the first Chairman.

Although the Tories found themselves back in office much sooner than Mr Chamberlain had anticipated, the Research Department had already justified itself. Mr Chamberlain wrote on 22 March 1930 :

... through my new department I shall have my finger on the springs of policy . . . we shall be at once an information bureau and a long-range research body . . . I am setting up a research into unemployment and out relief . . . I shall have another committee on over-production . . . another on social and in-dustrial problems, including thrift and co-partnership, and finally another on agriculture. I am particularly pleased with the latter, because hitherto all our investigations have simply endeavoured to find some vote-catching device.

Within the Conservative Party in the 1930s Mr Chamberlain probably initiated policy more than any other man. He put the Research Department on to systematic inquiries, instigated the formation of a publicity office which would be independent of local associations, and set on foot meetings of Conservative Ministers. He also found and encouraged a young and brilliant Conservative Member of Parliament who could develop party research. This was Mr R. A. Butler.

When Mr Chamberlain became Prime Minister he continued as Chairman of the Research Department, which then tended to become rather an instrument of his own. Sir Joseph Ball, the Department's Director, was very much a personal agent of Mr Chamberlain.

With the outbreak of war in 1939 it was decided to close the Research Department and release the staff for other work. But in fact the Department was revived from January to June 1940, not only to complete certain studies begun before the war, but also to handle and advise on some measures then in embryo – for example, the early proposals for Purchase Tax. Then it closed down again. When towards the end of the war social problems began to occupy the Government more and more, the need for a Research Department was felt acutely. But it proved too difficult to find men of the right calibre to staff it, and it was as much as the Party could do to provide Mr Henry Brooke, a former Deputy Director, with an office and a girl to assist him. These two managed as best they could until Mr David Clarke reappeared on the scene. For the General Election of 1945 the Department consisted of Mr Brooke, Mr Clarke and two secretaries.

After the 1945 Election, the most important task was to rally the Party and in particular to make the Parliamentary Party an effective Opposition. The Conservative Research Department played a great part in this.

In the organisation that I now joined in Old Queen Street I found some very stimulating companions. Mr Reginald Maudling, Mr Iain Macleod and Mr Enoch Powell all had their feet under desks there when they weren't pacing the carpet arguing with each other (though they never came to blows). Mr Maudling looked after economic affairs and drafted Mr Anthony Eden's speeches. Mr Powell busied himself with Defence in the widest connotation of the term. Mr Macleod was responsible for Home Affairs, including Health, on which he became such a master that after one speech when he got into the House in 1950 he was instantly earmarked to be Minister of Health.

It was a piece of great good fortune for me to fall in with this band of young men who were later to become some of the most influential people in the Conservative Party and in the public life of the country. Mr Butler was, of course, the chairman and he remained the chairman for very many years to come, both in and out of office. It was the wise and farsighted Rab who had recruited the outstandingly able young team who became my new friends.

Reggie Maudling in those days was a large and ample figure, though not quite as ample as he is now. In manner, he has remained unchanged through the years. He gave off then, as he still does, an air of indestructible calm, of unflappability, almost of idleness. In fact, he is a man of the keenest intellect; he has the sharpest and quickest of minds. I was greatly struck by his ability to hoist in detailed arguments. If you gave him a solid brief to be worked up into a speech, he would look at it in the morning and by evening would have produced a draft speech fit for a Privy Councillor.

Enoch Powell was one of the strangest – I might almost say bizarre – and attractive people that I had ever come

across. By now all the world is familiar with his attain-
ments : Greek scholar, poet and professor – and a brigadier
into the bargain. But all the world is not familiar with his
delightfully warm personal qualities, his friendliness and
charm. Enoch Powell is one of the most engaging people
that you could ever meet : in his personal relations gentle,
considerate, good-humoured and good-natured; in his
thinking utterly radical, fundamental and austere, getting
to the root of any subject that he examines. He was no
respecter of persons. One day in the Research Department
he received a letter from a senior member of the Party, a
Front Bencher. The statesman complained that he could
not understand the reason why the Research Department
had done something. From Powell he received the reply :
'There is a reason for everything.' Enoch Powell always
has thoughts of his own, and it is always stimulating to
hear them. He shocks at times by the strength of his
language as well as the originality of his thinking.

I should say myself – certainly this is how it seemed to
me at the time – that intellectually Maudling, Powell and
Macleod were all of a piece. There was little to choose
between them. In terms of ambition I might say the same
thing : they were all much of a muchness. They were all
determined to succeed in public life – and they all went on
to do so.

But the Celtic Macleod was unlike Maudling and Powell
in one important respect : he was less direct; he was more
subtle – though every bit as much fun to work with. I
remember once sitting with him in the Opposition Officials' Gallery during a House of Commons debate when I
nearly had to restrain him from leaping into the chamber
itself; he was so annoyed at what his own side was saying.
And this conviction, this confidence, has always been his

strength. He has always felt, I suspect, that he could do pretty well anything better than the next man. It can be a wonderfully helpful characteristic. Equally, it can be one of the most dangerous.

Presiding over these three apprentice statesmen, and over all the rest of us, was the established statesman, Mr Butler. Rab was already a political figure of the first importance. To me, still in my mid-twenties, he seemed totally immersed in politics. I could not imagine that he had any life outside politics. He appeared to be wholly engaged in public affairs. I found him rather grand and distant, but always courteous and considerate. In spite of his somewhat austere, indeed forbidding, public aspect, he is the kindest and most understanding of men.

Rab often worked from his own house in Smith Square, yet he knew about everything that went on in the Department. He was meticulously well informed about us all. This has always been true of Mr Butler. One of the astonishing things about him is his capacity for keeping tabs on people and affairs in whom and in which he is interested. He would startle one by saying something very pertinent to one's current activities, as if he had been in day-to-day contact with one. I found it slightly disquieting. One admired his exact knowledge of what was going on, yet wondered quite how the hell he did know.

The Director of the Department was then Mr David Clarke, a man of academic mould with a great grasp of the Party's history and policies. After a while Mr Clarke withdrew to the academic world, but he has now returned to the party's service as director of the Conservative College at Swinton.

Clarke and his successor, Michael Fraser, were equally able at running the Research Department. Fraser – now

Harold Macmillan, the author and his wife at the handing over of Petworth to the National Trust

Plate XIV

the eminent Sir Michael – had led a somewhat wild youth. He did well at Fettes and went from there with an Exhibition to study medicine at Cambridge. There he became somewhat of a tearabout – and an enthusiastic boxer until he discovered that it interfered with his social life. At the end of a year his Exhibition had been removed and he was in some danger of being sent down, but his tutor got him out of this. He went on to stay five years and in the fourth of these asked the same tutor for a sizeable loan to go abroad, and got it. He repaid this on promotion to Major after joining the Royal Artillery in the ranks on the outbreak of war. He first appeared at the Research Department as a young Lieutenant-Colonel in 1946 and directed the Department from 1951 to 1964.

What I liked about the Department was its camaraderie, the elasticity of its working hours, the loyalty of its staff to each other, and its bohemian sort of efficiency. We did not observe normal office hours. Sometimes I would be working very hard indeed – fourteen hours a day engaged on intensive cerebral work. One made up for this when times were slack by not turning up very early.

At that time I had a house in Chapel Street. I remember a rather pompous Conservative M.P. ringing me at the Research Department early one morning, wanting some information. The switchboard there, without letting on that I was not in the office, put him through to my house, where I happened to be in bed. I didn't know that the call had come through the office. The M.P., I supposed, knew that he was ringing me up at home. He, of course, thought that he was ringing me at the office. He asked me a number of questions which I was able to answer out of my head. He then asked me one which I could not answer, and I told him so. He said : 'Can't you go downstairs and look it up ?'

I said : 'What, in the kitchen?' He said : 'Do you mean to say that you have a kitchen there?' I said : 'Of course.' He said with heavy sarcasm : 'And I suppose you have a cook there too?' I said : 'That's right.' I rang off and then got up and went to the office. No doubt the M.P. went on believing to the end of his days that the Research Department worked in conditions of the utmost luxury. In fact we worked in Hogarthian but happy squalor at 24 Old Queen Street.

The main work of the Department in those years of Socialist Government was to provide ammunition for the Opposition and do drafting for the various official policy statements which the Party published. For example discussion at the Party Conference in 1946 had shown the need for a restatement of Conservative industrial policy. *The Industrial Charter* was published in May 1947. It was the first landmark on the road to our recovery in the realm of ideas. *The Agricultural Charter* was published in June 1948. It was a beacon for the Party on agricultural policy at that time. Most of the policies and production targets set out in it were subsequently achieved under Conservative Governments. *The True Balance*, about women's affairs, was published in February 1949. It was a flop, as political efforts to tackle specifically women's things usually are. *Imperial Policy*, published in June 1949, has not stood up well to the test of time, but it was nothing to be ashamed of. As for *The Right Road for Britain*, published in July 1949, it was the first Party statement since the war to cover the whole field of policy at home and abroad.

Endless detailed work was carried out by the Research Department day by day, as we answered inquiries, briefed members of both Houses, and interviewed national deputations. The Department were proud of their efforts. They only complained if these efforts were followed up by inadequate publicity and propaganda.

We really did have quite a good record of success. I remember in particular the famous meat debate.

By 1951 the meat ration had been reduced to 8*d* worth a week. On this subject, which affected everybody, and in anticipation of a Commons debate, I applied myself to some intensive work – coat off, slide-rule out (I am no good at sums, but I am a wizard with a slide-rule if I can count on somebody else to insert the decimal points in the right places).

The Opposition then put down a Motion on the Commons Order Paper:

in view of the mismanagement and lack of foresight shown in the supply of meat, whether home-produced or imported, and of the recent reduction in the weekly ration to the lowest level yet endured in this country, this House has no confidence in the capacity of His Majesty's Government to deal with the meat problem.

Before the debate I found that I had some arresting figures, and I gave them to Captain Harry Crookshank, who opened from the Opposition Front Bench. It is one thing to produce a massive and detailed brief, as I had done, but quite another to deploy it so effectively as to make a debate a great Parliamentary occasion – which is what Captain Crookshank did. I call this an illustration of the difference between the artisan and the artist.

Harry Crookshank was a small, trim man of great intelligence, courage and charm. He was well liked on both sides of the House. His intellectual ability was widely recognised, but he was thought to be on the idle side. He used to go about in a Rolls-Royce and lived with his sister in Pont Street.

Crookshank started off by saying that through the muddle of His Majesty's Government, His Majesty's lieges were reduced to eating the smallest ration of meat ever known in this country. The old Socialist, Mr David Kirkwood, rose to the fly by interjecting that Crookshank had never been hard up. A minute or two later he took the fly, interjecting again, saying that before the war the workers in his constituency did not see fresh meat for two years. Out came the brief. The 8*d* ration if taken in the most expensive form of steak represented about four ounces or about the size of a matchbox. If on the other hand it was taken in the form in which one got the most of the material, 'or whatever hon. Members like to call it', that comes from fat and antique ewe mutton, one could get about six ounces. The general average was about five ounces. Before the war this country was the largest meat-eating country in Europe except Denmark. Today it was on the lowest standard in Europe. There were shouts from Government supporters about the amount of meat that poor people had before the war. Very well, said Crookshank, what should we take as a comparison? The consumption of meat of a worker earning less than £5 a week? Or of men on unemployment benefit? Or what was given to people in workhouses? Or of men on the lower levels of wages, somewhere about 41*s*? Would the Government take their choice? Silence: there was no answer; everybody was rumbling from Crookshank's cocky demeanour that he had a cast-iron brief up his sleeve. There were loud shouts of 'Answer' from the Opposition benches. But still no answer came. Very well, said Crookshank, metaphorically rubbing his hands, as the other side was reluctant to make a choice, he would give the figures for all. In 1937–8, he said, families of people earning under

£5 a week consumed on the average twenty ounces of carcase meat per head per week. Our maximum in February 1951 – the highest possible maximum – was between five and six ounces. Then take the case of a family on 41s 8d a week, a husband, his wife and three children; they were purchasing just on eighteen ounces per head per week. An unemployed man with a wife and four children on benefit had 36s a week, and that family ate over nine ounces per head per week. Inmates in public assistance institutions had one pound of carcase meat a week, plus three and three-quarter ounces of corned beef – something like three times as much as the maximum that people could get in 1951. And so he went on.

Crookshank was a brilliant Opposition debater. Delighted with the Research Department's figures, he had gone down to the House that day with the express purpose of baiting the Government side. He did this with tremendous skill, trailing his coat and provoking so many noisy interruptions from the Government benches that the Speaker had to intervene. The quiet after Crookshank had shut them up was as dramatic as the noise which he had deliberately courted. He had started in an almost airy-fairy way giving the impression that, for somebody of his intellect and fastidiousness, having to make a speech on such a mundane subject as meat supplies was a distasteful task and an ephemeral effort, to be got out of the way and quickly forgotten. It was a remarkable scene and a remarkable performance. The Labour Government had expected an easy time. He had sailed into the debate like an elegant but harmless pleasure-yacht. Suddenly the ports had opened, his guns had been wheeled out and the other side had got some fearsome broadsides. Perhaps there are lessons in all this for every Opposition.

I recall only one comparable Opposition speech about that time – Iain Macleod's famous attack on the Minister of Health, the formidable Mr Aneurin Bevan. Macleod had left the Research Department to become a Member of Parliament. Whence had he got *his* ammunition? From the Conservative Research Department. Who had manufactured it? Iain Macleod when he was in the Department. Happy and rare the man in the complicated life of politics who achieves a great debating success which is all his own work.

It is much more fun being an attacker than a defender. To me, it was more fun being in the Research Department when the Party was in Opposition than it was after we returned to office in October 1951. But there was still much of interest to pursue.

One of the central difficulties of a party in office, when its leading members become absorbed in their duties as Ministers of the Crown, is to maintain and nourish adequate contact with their supporters up and down the country. Ministers are apt to get out of touch with the party at large. With this danger in mind, I pressed for the setting up of a Liaison Committee to provide a regular link between Government and Party. On 15 November 1951 I wrote a memorandum to Michael Fraser :

1. Over the years we built up the wide range of sources of information which has enabled us to answer almost any questions.

2. Conversely, we also received from these sources much useful and constructive advice which we transmitted to our front bench when the Party was in opposition.

3. At the same time, for example through Lord Swinton's committees – the Tactical Committee and (in General Elections) the Policy Committee – we were able to provide Mem-

bers, Candidates and others with up-to-date, informed advice on any topical questions.

4. Now that the Party is in power our contacts with our own front bench must necessarily be more remote. The Research Department would now hesitate about passing on suggestions to Ministers, unless Ministers asked for them. Ministers will look to their own civil servants. Yet ideas and suggestions will continue to flow into the Research Department; indeed even if they did not, the Research Department should be seeking them.

5. Nor is there any longer a service for dealing swiftly with questions of public interest as they arise. To give one small example, when the food cuts were announced, it was widely asked : why food, why not petrol, films, tobacco or wine ? These questions could have been anticipated and answered in advance.

6. In the years of opposition we (and Central Office) had achieved, by a process of evolution, the happy conditions under which everything could be dealt with expeditiously and, while much went into waste-paper baskets, nothing went into pigeon-holes.

7. Because of new circumstances we must have new arrangements.

8. These could be made very simply. My recommendation is that a clearing-house committee should be set up under the Chairmanship of Lord Swinton.

Fraser wrote to Mr Butler on 30 November 1951 :

There does, however, seem to be a great need for a 'clearing house' committee on the lines of that suggested by John Wyndham in a memorandum to me which I sent to you on 16th November. . . .

As you suggested at our meeting on 22nd November, I approached Lord Swinton about becoming Chairman of such a committee when I had a short meeting with him on Monday last. He considered the committee a good idea, but felt that he was too preoccupied at present to accept the chairmanship. He suggested that Lord Salisbury might be prepared to do so were a suitable approach made to him.

Both Central Office and the Research Department are now unable to deal expeditiously with Socialist propaganda, and the questions from our own supporters which inevitably result from it, because no regular channel exists, as it did before the General Election, between our own Front Bench and ourselves. As a result, there is an inevitable time lag during which the Socialists are able to make the whole of their case in the Press and elsewhere unchallenged. I am sure that this is doing us a great deal of harm in the constituencies, and that if allowed to continue it will affect adversely by-election results and the municipal elections in the spring.

Lord Swinton was eventually prevailed upon to become Chairman of the Committee, which met for the first time in his office at the Treasury on Friday, 21 December 1951. The original membership was Lord Swinton, Chancellor of the Duchy of Lancaster and Minister of Materials (Chairman); Mr Derick Heathcoat Amory, Minister of Pensions (Deputy Chairman); Mr John Hare, M.P., Vice-Chairman of the Conservative Party Organisation, with Lady Maxwell Fyfe, the other Vice-Chairman of the Party Organisation, as his alternative; Mr Angus Maude, M.P., Director of the Conservative Political Centre; Mr Mark Chapman-Walker, Chief Publicity Officer at Central Office; Mr Richard Greville, Personal Assistant to Lord Woolton; a representative of the Government Whips' office, who was an unknown young man called Edward Heath; and Michael Fraser. I was the secretary. The terms of reference were as follows:

To give guidance to Members of Parliament, candidates and others on the interpretation of Government policy and to take such action as, in their opinion, is necessary to sustain public confidence in the Conservative Administration.

As I wrote at the time, with stiff formality : 'The object of a Government should be, and should be seen to be, that each separate step which it takes is an integral part of a coherent general plan and not just one of a series of *ad hoc* expedients.' The object of the Liaison Committee was to pursue this path.

At the outset, it was then asked whether Members of Parliament should be informed that the Committee had been established. There were two views. Lord Swinton thought that the less publicity, the better. Mr John Hare argued, on the other hand, that in the 1922 Committee there had been pressure for machinery such as the Committee would provide. So it was decided to tell Members that this machinery was now in being.

I then drafted a letter for Lord Swinton to send to Ministers, and this he did. After setting out the Committee's terms of reference, and the membership, Lord Swinton went on :

The Committee will meet at least once a week, every Tuesday morning, in my room. It will have at its disposal the Party's existing media for putting across our case to the public – in particular, Talking Points similar to those which were produced for the guidance of Members and candidates when we were in Opposition and for which there has been a strong demand since the Election.

The main publicity for the Government must, of course, be done by the Government itself. What the Government does and says is news, whereas the Party Organisation can only present views.

But if Ministers can let the Party Organisation have background information, much of the 'follow up' publicity can be done by the Party Organisation, and in this way Socialist distortion can be combated.

At the same time, the Party Organisation has many means of

obtaining information about public opinion and the electorate's reaction to Government action. I hope that this Committee will be able to provide a channel of such information to Ministers.

The object of this letter is to seek help from Ministers in the guidance which the Committee will be giving on how policy measures should be understood. If Government decisions are to be properly explained to those who have to defend them in the country, the Committee will need comprehensive background advice, and I should be grateful to have my colleagues' views as to how the Committee can best be of service so far as the work of their own Department is concerned. In particular, I suggest it will be a great help to the Committee (and I think useful to Ministers) if, when a Minister is going to issue to the Press an announcement on a matter of policy or on a subject likely to have political reactions, the Secretary of the Committee can know in advance. The Committee felt that liaison could best be effected through Ministers' Private Secretaries, and, if you agree, Wyndham can get in touch with your Private Secretary.

The success of the Committee will, I believe, depend upon the sympathetic cooperation of Ministers. I know how difficult it is when we are all so hard pressed always to consider the psychological and Party aspects of our problems, but, with the hard times that lie before us and our narrow majority, it is essential that we should present our case in the best possible way. Within the field of the Party Organisation, that is what I hope this Committee will be able to do.

The Chief Whip has arranged for Mr Christ to devote himself specially to Lobby work and for this it is equally important that Christ should have constant contact with Ministers. The Chief Whip will be writing to you separately about this.

Mr Heath, still quite unknown, frequently spoke up at our meetings. Thus on 19 January 1952:

Item 4. *House Coal*

The Secretary reported that he had received an advance notice from the Minister of Fuel and Power's Private Secretary of the statement published in that morning's newspaper about house coal restrictions for February and March.

Mr Heath suggested that in clarity, terseness and content the statement compared favourably with that put out by the National Coal Board recently about coal prices. The severity of the rises in coal prices had come as a shock. It was generally agreed that the public had not clearly understood the reasons for them. Mr Fraser pointed out that the National Coal Board had in fact given the reasons. If those reasons had not got across, surely it was a case for 'follow up' publicity by the Party Organisation.

The Committee instructed the Secretary to ensure that adequate background material was promptly available to the Party Organisation when Boards issued announcements likely to have political repercussions.

I remember another meeting when we discussed an idea put forward by Mr Chapman-Walker, that when hard measures had to be announced the Government should at the same time announce some other and agreeable changes which would be well received by the public. In this way the Government might create a more favourable climate of opinion which, apart from considerations of popularity, might ensure more active support for their main policies. 'Blow-softeners' was what we had in mind. A very good idea too.

In all, I spent nearly five very happy – and I hope useful – years in the Research Department. Then in 1952 came the death of my Uncle Charles, Lord Leconfield, and I inherited his estates. I was obliged to leave the Research Department almost at once in order to deal with my new situation – which was pretty complicated. Thus I spent the next year or so at Petworth, attending to my personal affairs and learning about my new possessions, about which I shall have more to say later on.

Then, one day in 1955 when Mr Macmillan had become
Secretary of State for Foreign Affairs, he asked me over to
have lunch with him at Birch Grove. I motored across
Sussex to see my old master, and he said that he would like
me to rejoin him as one of his private secretaries in the
Foreign Office. By this time I was getting rather bored
with being a county councillor and a magistrate, and I
readily accepted his invitation.

So I went to work for him in the Foreign Office. Although my time at the Foreign Office was short, because
Mr Macmillan did not long remain there, I found it
altogether enjoyable – at times hilarious and at times odd.

We quite often had business with Sir Gladwyn Jebb,
then Ambassador in Paris, a person whom I much admired
and whom I have known for a long time. I always found
him expansive and charming, though his own subordinates
found him a bit of a handful. He is, of course, a brilliantly
clever man with somewhat masterful ways. The trouble
with Gladwyn is that he has a mind like a sausage-machine;
he churns stuff out inhumanly.

But nobody can be nicer than he when he wants to be.
He was particularly grand and apposite in the Paris Embassy, the old home of Princess Pauline Borghese,
Napoleon's sister. There is a picture of Pauline in the
Embassy. Seeing Gladwyn standing by it one morning, I
was struck by the resemblance. Could the tremendous
Bonaparte power, coupled with the beautiful Paris house
which we had taken over, really have had such an effect on
the incumbent Ambassador?

I accompanied Mr Macmillan to Geneva for a Foreign
Ministers' Conference. We stayed in a villa outside
Geneva. This was pleasant because one could occasionally
go out walking in the surrounding fields, where cows with

bells on their necks were making pretty noises. But most of the delegation were based on the Beau Rivage Hôtel in Geneva, and that was where the conference entertainment took place. The Russians, the French and the British all entertained each other in the same dining-room, with the same cook – and the same guests. It became a bit monotonous. Then I had a bright idea. We could not change the place or the people or the cooking, but we might change the ambiance. I rang up Gladwyn Jebb in his Paris Embassy and suggested that he should pile his beautiful gold plate into his Rolls-Royce and come to dinner with the Secretary of State at the Beau Rivage Hôtel in Geneva, where the plate would make a marvellous difference. Gladwyn showed no reluctance to come. He duly turned up with his plate, and we all dined by glorious candlelight glittering from his gold Embassy candelabra. He himself was sitting next to Molotov, the Soviet Foreign Minister. Gladwyn was pleased not only to be there, but also by his contribution to the décor. He expressed his feelings to Molotov. Molotov unfortunately has always had an acid sense of humour (if you can call it a sense of humour) – he is a man with a brilliant mind and a shrivelled soul, totally incapable of expansiveness or warmheartedness. Every joke of his has to be a snide one, and some of them fell rather flat that evening. When Gladwyn, proud of his gold plate and the glittering candles lighting up the dining-room, was dilating on the pretty scene, Molotov just sneered: 'In Moscow, we have the electric light.'

Mr Macmillan's principal private secretary at the Foreign Office, Patrick Hancock, was one of the cleverest and most charming, brisk and efficient men that I have ever met. He was also, if I may use an old-fashioned phrase, one of the straightest of men. He could not tell a lie.

One day he received a letter that obviously bothered him. He walked up and down his room in the Foreign Office looking rather *distrait* with this letter in his hand. I asked him what was the matter. He explained that it was a letter from somebody whom he had not seen since he was at Winchester, where the writer of the letter had bullied him terribly. Among other things, this bully had put Hancock in a trunk, knowing that he suffered from claustrophobia, and sat on the lid. The bully had grown up to become a clergyman, and now he was writing to Hancock from his deathbed. He was dying of cancer, apparently in agony. It appeared that he had only a few days to live. In the letter he was asking Hancock to send him an urgent message of forgiveness for all his bullying at Winchester. After he left school, he said, he had seen the light, and he had been troubled ever since by the wrong that he had done Hancock. Now, he asked only one thing – Hancock's forgiveness. He possibly had so short a time to live, he went on, that he would be grateful if Hancock would send him a message by telegram. This was why Hancock was so anguished. What should he do? It took him a good long time to decide, but having slept on it, he made his mind up. He despatched the following telegram: 'REGRET CANNOT FORGIVE (signed) HANCOCK.'

Just before Hancock got married to his nice wife, Beatrice, he announced his impending wedding in the Foreign Office and applied for leave, which was readily granted with congratulations. They asked him where he was going to spend it. He said in the Outer Hebrides. They said why the Hebrides? He said because he was mad about fishing. They said: 'But we all know that Beatrice loathes fishing.' He said: 'But Beatrice isn't coming.' They are still very happily married.

One of the things which has always endeared Mr Macmillan to me is his outward calm, whatever the turmoil within him; and this appearance of calm, whatever his real feelings, he always carried into his private office, thereby imparting it to others. In a way, he was like Queen Victoria, in that he always took it for granted that the chair would be there. By which I mean that Queen Victoria, when she paid a state visit to the Emperor Napoleon III and the Empress Eugénie, attended a state performance at the Paris Opéra. It was noticed that when the Empress Eugénie sat down, she looked round to see whether the chair was there. Queen Victoria did not.

Mr Macmillan was just the same. He took it for granted that the chair – or the speech – would always be there. He would never fuss, flap and worry beforehand – at any rate not outwardly. I have seen him many a time leave his room, at the Foreign Office or wherever, walk briskly out, get into his coat, and hold out his hand for the speech which he was about to make at the Lord Mayor's Banquet or whatever.

For many years I had two recurrent tiresome dreams. One was of missing early school at Eton. The other was of failing to deliver a speech into Mr Macmillan's hands at the right time. Alas, the latter dream came true. It was during the Foreign Ministers' Conference in Geneva. One day, in the middle of luncheon at the Foreign Secretary's villa, I rose to excuse myself saying that I wanted to make sure that Mr Macmillan's speech was in order before he went down to the Palais des Nations for the afternoon meeting. Kirkpatrick, the Permanent Head of the Foreign Office, said that there was no hurry because Mr Macmillan was due to speak last. Mr Macmillan told me to stop fussing and to sit down and finish my lunch: I could stay behind in the villa and bring the speech down when it was ready. I remained in the villa, checking the speech at leisure. But when all the Ministers were gathered together at the Palais des Nations, Molotov, who was due to speak first, said : 'I pass.' Dulles said the same. So did the French Foreign Minister. All eyes turned to Macmillan, who without looking round put his right hand behind him for his speech. But behind him was a vacant chair and no speech, no Wyndham. He withdrew his empty hand, feeling more amazement – as I learned later – than he showed on his face, and straight away suggested that the Foreign Ministers should adjourn for refreshment. Next thing, of course, a great hue and cry for me, and I dashed down with the speech. The moral is that a private secretary should always have a speech ready when it is needed and not when other people, no matter how grand, think that it may be needed.

Mr Macmillan was not long at the Foreign Office, and I am sure that he regretted this. He would have liked to stay longer, to make a name for himself as a great Foreign Secretary. But, as things turned out, he was there no more than eight months. The Prime Minister, Sir Anthony Eden, then decided on certain changes in the Government, and he invited Mr Macmillan to take over the Treasury in succession to Mr Butler. Rab was at this time in low spirits. He had not recovered from the terrible blow of his wife's death, and he was in need of a change. The Prime Minister understood this.

Mr Macmillan first heard of the proposed transfer just as he was about to leave London on an official journey abroad. He received the news in a letter from the Prime Minister which he read in the V.I.P. lounge at London Airport. In this Mr Eden told Mr Macmillan what he had in mind, and he added that he was proposing to designate Mr Butler Deputy Prime Minister. Mr Macmillan was unwilling to leave the Foreign Office, but nevertheless he accepted his new appointment with good grace. He did not, however, concur with the Prime Minister in thinking that Rab should be designated Deputy Prime Minister, and he lost no time in telling Eden so. The proposal was abandoned.

And so Mr Macmillan now moved away to the Treasury. But I couldn't go with him, for personal and unique reasons. I had to retire again because I was myself in dispute with the Treasury over death duties, and the Treasury was the last department of state in which I could possibly work. Thus I retired to Petworth for the second time – there to continue my battle with the department of which my old friend and master was now the head. I may say that Mr Macmillan himself, on becoming Chancellor, refused to handle my affairs. Indeed he said so in a letter :

17th September, 1956

My dear John,

I rang you up the other day but found you were in Venice. I hope you had a very good time there. I had a talk with your mother who told me that you would be coming back very soon. Meanwhile I thought I ought to tell you that I have asked Henry Brooke to take charge of the negotiations regarding the pictures, and to try and bring the matter to a conclusion. I thought it was wiser for me not to manage it myself for fear that you or I might be accused by ill-disposed persons. But it is a great grief to me that it has gone on so long, and I will do my best to see that Henry brings it to a conclusion as soon as he can. I am going to America on Thursday, but shall be back in ten days. I hope to see you again soon.

Yours ever

HAROLD

L

It was for these reasons that I found myself at Petworth during the months when Suez was building up and events were leading to Eden's resignation and Mr Macmillan's emergence as Prime Minister.

In 1789 there was a Marquis de l'Aigle who snapped his fingers at the French Revolution and went on hunting at Compiègne. This, more or less, was what I was doing at the time of Suez – though I was actually trying to improve the estate. Certainly people at Petworth seemed keen on the operation and disappointed at its failure.

So was I and so were most of my friends. Tempers ran high at the time. For example, in the circle of friends to which I belong the Astor family have long been held in great affection. But at the time of Suez various members of that family were dead against it, and the cry went up from some of us : 'Astors, go home.'

As I say, I was involved in my country pursuits and knew no more than I saw in the newspapers. From what I read I deduced that there was something phoney going on, however. All the talk about the British and French going in to separate the Israelis and the Egyptians. . . . I didn't believe a word of it. But, rightly or wrongly, I decided that I didn't object if it resulted in regaining the Canal. I thought that the two things were not incompatible anyway. Well, we all know what happened.

Came January 1957 and the resignation of Sir Anthony Eden. I myself expected Mr Butler to succeed him. I had not foreseen that the new Prime Minister would be Mr Macmillan. Like pretty well everybody else (except Mr Randolph Churchill) I was wrong.

I heard afterwards that when Anthony Eden announced his resignation to the Cabinet appropriate tributes of affection and sorrow were paid to him by Rab Butler and

Harold Macmillan, after which Eden withdrew. The rest of the Cabinet, on filing out, were stopped by Sir Norman Brook, the Cabinet Secretary, who asked them to go, one by one, into another room where Lord Salisbury and Lord Kilmuir were seated at a table. This pair interrogated their colleagues on the succession. They thought it best, they said, that there should be no discussion. What they wanted was a straight answer to the question: 'Who's best – Rab or Harold?' They got it.

CHAPTER SIX

Private Office

THUS on 10 January 1957 Mr Macmillan became Prime Minister. He was sixty-two years of age.

His early months were given over almost entirely to picking up the pieces after Suez and trying to restore the broken morale of the Conservative Party. He was up against it. But because everything seemed loaded against him he was at his very best. His friends found him full of fight and spirit and fun and gaiety. He thrived in adversity.

It was no easy passage, however. Mr Macmillan had plenty of troubles – among them Lord Salisbury. Lord Salisbury had resigned before I returned to Mr Macmillan's service. He had offered his resignation over Cyprus. To Lord Salisbury's astonishment, Mr Macmillan had accepted it. Archbishop Makarios, who had incurred strong feeling against himself because he was suspected of being far too much mixed up with Enosis, had been exiled to the Seychelles. When it came to the question of bringing him back, Lord Salisbury cut up rough in Cabinet. But he lost the tussle. Most Ministers were in favour of Makarios's release. Lord Salisbury then asked to see Mr Macmillan and had a talk with him in his small sitting-room upstairs in No. 10. The Prime Minister would not budge. Makarios, he said, was going to be released and returned to Cyprus.

Whereupon Lord Salisbury, very upset, tendered his resignation, and in those years at Downing Street there was probably nothing to equal the astonishment when Mr Macmillan accepted it. Why did the Prime Minister do it? He did it because he thought that he would not be in office much longer and, while he was there, he was determined to show who was the boss. He was not prepared, as chairman of the board, so to speak, to go back at the behest of another director and try to make the board change its mind. He explained all this to Lord Salisbury, who still remained adamant. Very well, said Mr Macmillan, you will have to go. So Lord Salisbury went. I do not know quite how much this upset Lord Salisbury, but I do know that it upset Mr Macmillan. The two had been friends for many years.

It was four and a half months after he became Prime Minister that I rejoined Mr Macmillan. My recall to his service began with a letter which he sent to me from the Palace of Holyroodhouse on 27 May 1957:

Dear John,

During the last few months I have hesitated whether I would venture to write to you about the chance of your being willing to rejoin the old firm – in some capacity or other, on a full- or half-time basis. The fact is that I did not really think my administration could last more than a few weeks; but we seem now to have got over quite a number of jumps in this Grand National course, and having just managed to pull the old mare through the brook and somehow got to the other side with the same jockey up, and the Cecil colours fallen, I am plucking up my courage. Would you at any rate come and talk to me about it? I know our team at No. 10 would like very much to have you with them, and I think there are certain aspects of my work where you could really be a great help to me. Anyway, will you give them a ring

and fix up to come and see me the next time you are in London ?
If you could both come to lunch, it would be best, but if not,
some other free time.

Yours ever,

H.M.

This is one of the most remarkable letters that I have
ever received. Mr Macmillan's admission that at the outset
he did not really expect his administration to last more
than a few weeks, and the buoyant optimism that he was
now displaying four and a half months later, is as revealing
as anything that he could have written.

And so I joined him again. I met my future colleagues to
fix up the job. They asked what conditions I had in mind to
make. They were a bit surprised when I quoted them the
story of the Duc d'Aumale and Sarah Bernhardt. The Duc
sent her a message from his box in the theatre where she
was acting : 'Ou, quand, combien?' In the interval Sarah
sent back a note : 'Chez moi, ce soir, pour rien.'

I was welcomed into the Private Secretaries' circle and
so it went on until Mr Macmillan ceased to be Prime
Minister.

Thus my life and arrangements changed yet again. I was
living then in a house in Cowley Street, Westminster,
which I rented from Lord Head, who was serving abroad
as a High Commissioner. Whenever I think of Anthony
Head and his delightful wife I am reminded of a nice little
story. His wife, Lady Dorothea Ashley-Cooper, known to
her friends and relations as Dot or Dottie, was the daughter
of Lady Shaftesbury, who was at the Court of King
George V and Queen Mary. Queen Mary was devoted to
Lady Shaftesbury. Lady Shaftesbury was affectionately
known to her friends as Cuckoo. One day Lady Shaftesbury
told Queen Mary that she was very excited because two of

her daughters were expecting children. Queen Mary expressed great interest and hoped that Lady Shaftesbury would let her know as soon as she had good news. Dot Head gave birth to a child, and a telegram was immediately sent by Lady Shaftesbury to the Queen announcing the happy fact that Lady Shaftesbury was a grandmother. Queen Mary sent back a congratulatory message which ended with the inquiry as to which daughter it was. Back along the electric wires came the splendid message: 'DOTTIE, MA'AM. (signed) CUCKOO.' This gave the postmaster at Buckingham Palace something to think about.

My days with the Prime Minister used to begin with an early if hasty reading of all the newspapers, while I was still in bed. I had to do this because Mr Macmillan got tomorrow's newspapers the night before – that is to say he received the first editions about 11 o'clock on the eve of publication. He was therefore one up on me, and would often ring up early in the morning and say: 'Have you seen that bit by Marks in the *Daily Express*?' If I hadn't, there was a tremendous temptation to lie and say: 'You've got the early edition. There's nothing by Marks in my edition.' But I never actually said it. Much too dangerous.

I would then get up and take the only exercise of the day by walking from Cowley Street to No. 10.

The amazing thing about 10 Downing Street for anybody with a sense of atmosphere was that when you entered that celebrated door and were inside, perhaps expecting a heavy air of leaden responsibility, you found instead a surprising calm. This was at all events my own experience in Mr Macmillan's day. Perhaps it was because there is always calm in the middle of a cyclone. Or perhaps it was because 10 Downing Street, besides being the

Prime Minister's office, was also his home, and the visitor might meet on arrival one of Mr Macmillan's small grandsons playing in the hall with a Government messenger or a dog or a toy motor-car. No. 10 is a private house as well as the centre of government, and it is all the more attractive for that.

From the hall you go down a long white passage, lined with busts of previous Prime Ministers, to a lobby in which at a round table, when there is a Cabinet meeting, you discover a covey of Ministers not in the Cabinet. They are Ministers or Parliamentary Secretaries understudying for Cabinet Ministers who cannot attend, waiting to be called into the Cabinet when their subject comes up.

This must be one of the most wretched duties for any junior member of a government. He is left kicking his heels in the lobby until the Cabinet reach his item on the agenda. Then he is sent for, invariably to find that the Cabinet have already started discussing his subject; and, from the glazed eyes before him as he begins saying his piece, he soon realises that somebody else has already said it.

Most Cabinets consist of some twenty-odd members. It seems a potty way to run a business. To my mind, the number should be cut to a dozen. The method of work and the arrangement of meetings should also be changed. As it is, the Cabinet go on with the matters in hand until the clock on the chimneypiece under Walpole's portrait says one o'clock, whereupon the general consensus of opinion is: 'Oh-well-it's-one-o'clock-let-us-meet-again-on-Thursday.'

In my day, every paper or letter addressed to the Prime Minister was sieved either by his confidential clerks or by the 'Garden Rooms'. The Garden Rooms were called the Garden Rooms because they faced the garden of No. 10.

These Garden Rooms were occupied by a number of lady assistants who worked and typed on a 24-hour rota for the Prime Minister and his private secretaries. They were the most diligent team imaginable.

On the floor above the Garden Rooms were the Cabinet Room and the office of the Prime Minister's private secretaries. The private secretaries occupied two rooms which were really one room because the door in between had been removed.

From time to time theorists write about how the system of government might be reformed. Most of these writings are bad; bad generally are those by retired civil servants; worse are those by retired temporary civil servants. The main reason is that the civil service is changing all the time and civil servants still at work are inhibited from writing about it – rightly so.

The circumstances in which they work alter rapidly from government to government and minister to minister and from year to year. In my experience, the civil servants adapt themselves marvellously well. Because he is bound to be behind the times, the ex-insider, now outside, should be very careful in what he says about the machine which is changing all the while.

One of the most interesting things about Mr Macmillan when he had got to the top as Prime Minister, after an apprenticeship as hard as most of us would wish to avoid, was his gentleness. You might have thought that by that time he would subconsciously have sought to work out of his system the previous long years of frustration by throwing his weight about. Well, he didn't, even though he was the most powerful Prime Minister since Churchill and held office without a break longer than any man since Asquith. He was always polite, courteous and outwardly calm, and he was very quick in getting through his work.

What makes No. 10 tick? The people there are highly intelligent and will respect a highly intelligent master and do their very best for him whether they like him or not. Mr Macmillan when he was Prime Minister was not only respected but liked.

The main reason why things worked well, when they did, was I think that Mr Macmillan would say what he wanted to be done and tell others to get on with it. If you simply ask civil servants on any given subject what they think about it, you are apt to waste everybody's time. They form little *ad hoc* committees and produce papers of the on-the-one-hand-but-on-the-other sort. If instead you say what you want done, they are likely to find a good way of doing it.

Mr Macmillan when Prime Minister had four private secretaries. They changed from time to time. While it is not my object to read a full roll-call of these splendid and devoted lieutenants, among those who served him in turn were Freddie Bishop, who has since left the public service to better himself with Whitehall Securities, Tim Bligh, who has since left to better himself with Lord Thomson, Philip de Zulueta, who has since left to better himself with Hill, Samuel, and Neil Cairncross, Anthony Phelps and Philip Woodfield, who still shine in the civil service.

If you had given the Macmillan private secretaries a whelk-stall to run, you could have been sure that in a very short time they would have collared the whole of the whelk business. And they were extremely loyal. But the point is that the Prime Minister had only four young men on whom to depend. Other Ministers presided over great Departments with all the apparatus which they command. If you

are an ambitious Minister, it is important for you to be a
Minister with a great Department behind you. The resounding titles like Lord President of the Council and
Lord Privy Seal are as sounding brass or a tinkling cymbal
because they are without large Departments. The Minister
in charge of a great Department is a magnate while he
holds his office, with power over a lot of people. Ministers
like the Lord President of the Council and the Lord Privy
Seal – not to speak of that lower form of ministerial life,
the Minister without Portfolio – unless very special func-
tions have been allocated to them sit sadly in little offices
with their private secretaries and nobody else. The others
tend to pass them by. The Prime Minister is in a like
position except for the fact that he has the hiring and the
firing of his ministerial colleagues, which does make a
difference. Nevertheless he may very well ache to collar a
Department for himself and thus expand the horizon of his
office beyond his four young men, the private secretaries.
In the war, Winston Churchill collared the Ministry of
Defence. In 1967, Mr Wilson collared the Department of
Economic Affairs. The Cabinet Office is no use for this
purpose, for the Cabinet Office exists to look after the
Cabinet as a whole and not just the Prime Minister. It
would be against its nature to become the creature of one
man, *primus inter pares* though he is.

Mr Macmillan, because of his seniority both in years and
experience, and because, despite that gentleness of manner,
he was capable of being ruthless – as were his small staff –
managed to interfere time and time again with Ministries
over the heads of various Ministers.

Sometimes this riled other Ministers. I remember being
with him in the Grand Hotel at Scarborough for a Conservative Party Conference when a labour dispute was

going on. He telephoned the Ministry of Labour and spoke to various officials in detail and in no uncertain terms. Mr John Hare, the Minister of Labour (he is now Lord Blakenham), spoke to me about this afterwards. Who, he asked, was the Minister of Labour, himself or the Prime Minister? Well, of course, I did my best to calm him down, and I hope succeeded.

In any Prime Minister's office there is obviously a great volume and variety of business. If the private office is to work properly, each member of it should be familiar with what the others are doing. There has to be a full and methodical exchange of information between them without wasting each other's time.

We were all of us sharpening our minds on one another, walking from one room to the other, pacing the floor and deliberating the business in hand. Mr Macmillan made it a rule that the work which flowed in during the course of the day had to be dealt with by his private secretaries during that day unless there was a good reason for delay.

The Prime Minister himself used to wake up early in the morning and straight away he would attack a huge box of papers consisting of submissions put up to him by his private secretaries the night before. This box had stood on a table in the private secretaries' room the day before, and the private secretaries during that day had dropped their submissions into it. As the day wore on, the box got fuller. The great crime was not to know what was in the box. The box was closed at the end of business by the private secretary on late duty and given to a messenger, who then put it in the Prime Minister's bedroom.

When we came in next morning the box would be back downstairs with succinct comments by the Prime Minister on each submission. We all got to know Mr Macmillan so well that the shortest of notes by him would often suffice. For example: 'Tell him No. H.M.' One would then write:

The Prime Minister has asked me to thank you very much for your kind letter. He is most grateful to you for the trouble you took in writing as you did. Much as he would like to do as you ask, he regrets that the pressure of work and events obliges him to decline. He is very sorry to have to send you this disappointing reply, but he is sure that you will understand how he is placed. He wishes me to take this opportunity to send on his behalf his best wishes, etc., etc.

For good measure there was also a thing known as the Dip. This consisted of carbon copies of all the letters and minutes written the day before, and it was in the hands of the confidential clerks, one of whom always sat in my room. It was called the Dip because we dipped into it to keep ourselves *au fait*. So nobody had any excuse for not knowing what the others were up to.

Harold Macmillan also made me keep a box at No. 10 called the Bits and Pieces Box. This was an idea that he had borrowed from Sir Winston Churchill. Into this box we put unused quips and any other good passages which had not been reported in his previous speeches, and any ideas that might come in handy for future speeches.

Not the least efficient part of the No. 10 set-up was the switchboard, manned – or rather womanned – by some admirable ladies from the General Post Office. They took a great pride in their work, and did it with unbelievable speed. I remember one or two occasions when Mr Macmillan was engaged in Cabinet-making. When a Prime Minister is reconstructing his government there is not much time to be lost. Perhaps he wishes to offer a job to Mr X, and if Mr X refuses then he is going to offer it to Mr Y. But it is important that both X and Y should be –

and should be known to be – within reach. I recall that when Anthony Eden was forming his government, he wished to get in touch with a Mr Y. The switchboard were told to get hold of him, but not to disclose who wanted him. They did this successfully after a little delay. They subsequently apologised for the hold-up, explaining that they had had to get him out of Bertram Mills's Circus at Olympia, which he was attending (of course as a spectator) at the time.

As I say, Mr Macmillan used to wake up early and do his box, which his private secretaries would find waiting for them in their room when they came in. He would stay in bed as long as possible, thinking or drafting, or sending for his private secretaries and giving them instructions. He had a very good cook called Mrs Bell and a housemaid called Edith, and one often had dealings with both of them. 'Edith, where is the Prime Minister? I have just been up to his bedroom and he isn't there. Have you let him escape?' 'No, he is in the bathroom.' 'Well, let me know when he comes out because I want to see him.' 'Very well.' 'Mrs Bell, the Prime Minister says I have got to come to lunch with him today. Is that all right?' 'Oh, very well.'

My chief impression of the private office at No. 10 was of absolute calm. The calmest element of all was Mr Macmillan. Anybody who got excited got short shrift. Mr Macmillan's great relaxation was reading. However serious the crisis, once he had decided that there was nothing more to do about it, he would retire to his study and read. We were welcome to go in at any time nevertheless. He would then discuss the problem and return to his reading. He had a wonderful gift of switching his mind on and off. This is probably the secret of his great physical stamina, damaged

10, Downing Street,
Whitehall.

Motto for Private Office
+ Cabinet Room
———

Quiet, calm deliberation
disentangles every Knot.
———

HM

though his body had been by three wounds in the 1914–18 war. He took great care of himself. His doctor, Sir John Richardson, called on him once a month. His only relaxations were reading, pottering about and shooting.

All the Prime Minister's secretaries had scrambler telephones in their homes so that he could speak to them, in some sort of security, at any time. In No. 10 there was the famous direct line to the White House, and various other intricate communications systems. The White House telephone was a red instrument, and it was wheeled in, when needed, on a sort of tea-trolley. Plugged in, it connected Downing Street and the White House almost at once.

The so-called special relationship with the United States – when it operated, how it operated and when it ceased, if it ever did – will be an interesting subject for future historians when all the archives can be released for study.

Churchill, when Prime Minister and even before, forged a special relationship with President Roosevelt. They were great friends. Think of all those intimate and secret telegrams from Churchill to the President in the war and Roosevelt's warm responses. It was a great friendship, and they could both be very gay together. At a picnic in Morocco in the middle of the war, I remember them happily reciting lines from Omar Khayyam as they toasted each other :

> Here with a Loaf of Bread beneath the Bough,
> A Flask of Wine, a Book of Verse – and Thou.

President Roosevelt called Churchill 'Winston', which was natural enough. But Churchill, with his innate sense of protocol, always addressed Roosevelt as 'Mr President', because the President was a Head of State and Churchill

Back to the land: auctioning a prize steer and encouraging Cumberland slate-workers

Lady Egremont talking to Mr Spencer in the Grinling Gibbons Room

was not. President Kennedy addressed Mr Macmillan as 'Prime Minister' – no doubt out of respect for an older person. I venture to say that the confidence between Mr Macmillan and President Kennedy was the greater.

Macmillan was impressed by the charm, ability and toughness of the young President. The President on his side was impressed by Macmillan's wisdom and sheer experience. They had a family link in the fact that the President's sister Kathleen had been married to Macmillan's nephew, Lord Hartington, who was killed in the war. They used to speak to each other very often on the red telephone. These telephone conversations were monitored at both ends by the respective staffs. The intimacy between Prime Minister and President occasionally caused some confusion. I recall one conversation when the President said : 'We're looking forward to having Debo here.' After the conversation had ended the White House staff rang us up to check that we had heard it all clearly. Yes, we said. So had they, they said – but what was this new outfit called DEBO? SEATO, CENTO, NATO and what not they knew. Now, as they understood the conversation, DEBO was going to be set up in Washington.

We explained that it was Deborah, Duchess of Devonshire, Kathleen's sister-in-law, who was coming to stay in Washington for a few days.

Mr Macmillan seldom showed his feelings. His face was as impassive as Talleyrand's is said to have been. But when he was working in the Cabinet room, and if you happened to drop a pencil on the floor, you would discover his mood while you were bending down to pick up the pencil. You could then observe what the Prime Minister's feet were doing; if they were drumming on the floor, you were going about the business in the wrong way. When

M

he was in bed, of course, you had no means of knowing.

You never knew, as you approached 10 Downing Street, what you were going to find when you got there. One morning, when I went in, I was told that the Prime Minister had been asking for me. I went up to his bedroom. 'What am I going to do about this horse?' he asked. He noticed the puzzled look on my face and said: 'Don't you read the Foreign Office telegrams?' The penny dropped. I realised that he was talking about a horse which a foreign potentate was proposing to present to him. I said not to bother: I would deal with the matter and, if need be, accommodate the horse at Petworth.

As a matter of fact I was rather looking forward to riding that horse. But the Ministry of Agriculture, when I told them about it, said that if the horse came, it would have to be shot on the quay – African Horses' Disease. The potentate, when we had conveyed this to him, said very well, he would bring two gazelles instead. As the owner of four hundred head of fallow deer, I would have been quite happy to make a bit of a change at home by accommodating gazelles. But the Ministry of Agriculture again stepped in, quoting a regulation about ungulate ruminants. The potentate gave it up and brought nothing – thereby saving everybody a lot of trouble.

Wordsworth sang:

> A primrose by a river's brim
> A yellow primrose was to him
> And it was nothing more.

To some of us a gazelle is just a gazelle and nothing more; but to the Ministry of Agriculture it is an ungulate ruminant.

There was always a neatness about Mr Macmillan

which became more and more apparent as he grew older. The moustache became more trim. There was never a grey hair out of place on that fine head. Those sensitive hands were always immaculate. But he was never a dandy, and Lady Dorothy used to worry about his clothes. His suits were old, though carefully looked after by Edith, the housemaid. He could not be bothered to go to the tailor. He was not like the younger Pitt, who when Prime Minister and heavily in debt to both his coachmaker and his tailor, and severely pressed for payment, always ordered another carriage and another suit. Harold Macmillan could afford these things but didn't bother about them. The Prime Ministerial cars were small.

His neatness showed itself in his way of arranging his many books, so that he always knew where to find one, and in the way in which he arranged his sitting-room at No. 10. Everything was in apple-pie order. On the chimneypiece there was a photograph of his father and another of the Scottish croft whence the Macmillans came. The desk was always tidy, with no papers lying about except the one on which he was actually working at the time. Unlike many politicians, he never mislaid a paper. I don't mean that politicians habitually lose papers, but with some Ministers it takes time to find them again. Mr Macmillan always knew where everything was or ought to be.

He drank very little before luncheon, but when he did it was a gin and tonic or a glass of sherry. With luncheon he drank scarcely anything, but in the evenings he would usually take a glass or two of whisky before dinner and wine at dinner. He liked port – also champagne if he had someone to share it with him. During Lent he gave up drink altogether.

Mr Macmillan is the most considerate of men. He always

looks after his guests properly. And he always looked after his colleagues if they were doing business with him in the evening. Before their meeting he would see that whisky was put out for them. But he seldom drank a drop before making a speech.

He ate very little. For breakfast he usually had tea and toast and an occasional boiled egg. At luncheon his favourite dish was cold roast beef. Dinner was a bore for him. This was a very sound regime. But he did occasionally break out. On one famous occasion, as we all know, he was found dining off oysters and steak with Mr Edward Heath. He was and remains a clubbable man. He belongs to a good many clubs – and he visits them all. But he is greatly missed in the smoking room of one club from which he resigned – the smoking room of the House of Commons.

Mr Macmillan was the best speechmaker off the cuff whom I have ever known. He could stand up and make an impromptu speech with a beginning and, what is much more difficult, a tidy end. While he was Prime Minister he was, as I thought, unnecessarily chary of making speeches off the cuff for fear that he might say something which he would later regret. As time went on, however, he became more confident. He was in any case much too much of an old hand to drop a clanger. His usual custom when about to address a large public meeting was to invite the Conservative Research Department, in collaboration with Mr George Christ of the Conservative Central Office, to provide him with a draft. This he would then revise and go through over and over again, draft after draft – there would probably be about seven drafts – with Sir Michael Fraser of the Research Department and George Christ and me in the Cabinet room.

How good Mr Macmillan was off the cuff I first discovered in 1957, when he went to address the annual
meeting of the Institute of Directors at the Festival Hall in
London. I had, after consultation with others, prepared a
draft speech for him at a time when he was particularly
busy. He had read through the draft and had written on it :
'This will do.' But on the morning of the day, and having
devoted more thought to it, he told me that my draft was
bad and he could not use it. What were we to do? He
decided to go and speak off the cuff. His speech was a
tremendous success, but like all good speeches better said
than read.

I came to realise that the manufactured speeches which
Mr Macmillan used after they had gone through so many
hands were never so good as the pure undiluted Mac-
millanism. I therefore adopted a subterfuge. When he was
going to make a speech off the cuff which was not to be
reported, I arranged for a recording device to be installed.
The record was a wonderful basis for the next speech.

Black boxes with papers in them were the basis of our
operations when on the move, which we frequently were.
Mr Macmillan as Prime Minister travelled to France,
Russia, Germany, Pakistan, India, Ceylon, Singapore, New
Zealand, Australia, Ghana, Nigeria, Zambia, Malawi,
Rhodesia, South Africa, the West Indies, Canada and the
United States. On all these journeys he was accompanied
by a quantity of black boxes with his papers in them.
Wherever he went his private office was set up and was
going full-swing twenty minutes after arrival. We
reckoned that, if need be, we could snap up all the black
boxes and encase the typewriters and be off again at
twenty minutes' notice.

On these journeys we were accompanied by two cypher

clerks. On one of the Commonwealth tours, when we were at the back of beyond somewhere in Australia and being badgered by a correspondence with Mr Khrushchev, I explained to a distinguished Australian that we were a bit pushed but were managing all right despite the big telegram load. The Australian was full of admiration about the way in which we were coping, but wondered how we despatched our telegrams. Had we got some secret wireless transmitter with us? He was rather surprised when I said that no, after they had been encyphered in an unbreakable cypher, we took the telegrams round to the local Post Office, who then despatched them very efficiently.

I was at Downing Street for the resignation of the Chancellor of the Exchequer, Mr Peter Thorneycroft, and his two lieutenants at the Treasury, Mr Enoch Powell and Mr Nigel Birch. It was unprecedented that all the Treasury Ministers should resign together. The three of them had been muttering to each other for some time about re-signing over rising government expenditure, and suddenly they found a splendid opportunity for putting a pistol to the Prime Minister's head. This was the occasion of Mr Macmillan's departure for a long tour of the Commonwealth (India, Pakistan, Ceylon, Singapore, Australia, New Zealand) lasting several weeks. No sooner had the tour been completely arranged and the date of the departure announced with the dates of arrival in the various capitals, than they addressed themselves directly to the Prime Minister. They had now stopped muttering to each other; they were muttering to him.

Some of Mr Macmillan's private secretaries, getting wind of what the Chancellor and his colleagues had in mind, had ventured to suggest to Mr Thorneycroft that their behaviour was perhaps not what it ought to be. Mr

Thorneycroft looked embarrassed but took the line that the short time available would enable Mr Macmillan to concentrate his mind on the issue in dispute. Only a day or two before the Prime Minister was due to leave London he received letters of resignation from all three. All the letters arrived at once.

As it happened, I was the last private secretary to reach the private office that morning and, having bidden everybody good morning, I noticed that the atmosphere was more piano than usual. Cairncross said: 'We just have a little matter of these three letters on our hands' and showed me copies. The originals had already gone upstairs to Mr Macmillan. The Chief Whip, Mr Edward Heath, was, of course, sent for.

Mr Macmillan appeared on the scene, walking in looking calm and benign: 'Ah, my dear John, there you are. And Pamela, is she all right? And my godson Max: how is he getting on? Well, I hope? And your other son – what's his name – how is he? Enjoying himself in the country, I trust?' And so on round the room. A studied act. And then he made a little joke or two and said now we must get down to business, and went into the Cabinet room where he was followed by a private secretary or two. He then spent what seemed an inordinate time discussing slowly and calmly any amount of trivialities, occasionally ringing a bell for a secretary and dictating a totally unimportant letter. After which he became rather serious and terse.

Letters accepting the resignations were quickly drafted and Mr Macmillan said that he was about to travel many thousands of miles and the line was that this was to be treated as a little local difficulty. The expression became famous. He had made his mind up; he was clear that this was how it was to be treated, and so it was.

So off we went on the Commonwealth tour, and we were greeted with friendliness and hospitality everywhere. There was a great welcome in Delhi, where Mr Nehru put on a show for Mr Macmillan's arrival. I remember a man breaking from the cheering crowd and running alongside Mr Macmillan's car shouting : 'Once you were our masters; now you are our friends.' From India we went to Pakistan, where we met with equal kindness, as everywhere on the tour.

These tours are wearing. We reached Delhi in time for lunch after a night and a morning in the aeroplane. The chief trouble about shooting around the world in aeroplanes is the effect which differing times in differing countries have on one's inside. On arrival in Delhi the kindly and hospitable Indians for our sake broke their non-drinking rules and offered me a whisky and soda, which I gratefully accepted. No sooner had I taken a sip than I felt a feeling of nausea because by stomach-time it was 8.30 a.m.

In Australia it was reported that my wife had given birth to a child. I was so weary that when a kindly lady said : 'Is it a boy or a girl?' I was only able to say : 'I hope so.'

But the tour was a huge success and was one of several which Mr Macmillan made round the Commonwealth. It was a success in three senses. They liked seeing him. He liked seeing them. And this shy, Celtic man, possibly for the first time since he had mingled with the unemployed in the narrower confines of Stockton-on-Tees, found tremendous welcomes for him everywhere and responded to them with open-hearted charm, stopping his car and getting out and talking to people, to their immense delight.

Harold Macmillan is a most curious person. He was always a mixture of shyness, zest and ability. Zest does not usually go with shyness, but it did with him until this tour, when he found himself at last by walking about in crowds and realising that he could dominate them quite naturally, always making the apposite remark, saying the right thing.

Driving one evening through a city in Australia he stopped his car, got out and walked into the crowd and said to an Australian: 'Why aren't you in the pubs?' The Australian replied: 'Because they've just closed.' Mr Macmillan then delighted all within earshot by saying that if only the rules about opening pubs in Britain and Australia were combined, they would be open all the time. He then got back into his car and drove on amid cheers.

Next there was his tour of Africa – the so-called 'Wind of Change' tour. The 'Wind of Change' speech was made by Mr Macmillan to a joint meeting of the two Houses of the South African Parliament in the presence of the South African Prime Minister, Dr Verwoerd. I was not there when Mr Macmillan spoke. Instead, I listened to his speech on the wireless with Mrs Verwoerd at Groote Schuur, Cecil Rhodes's old home. Mr Macmillan, in fact, said nothing which should have seemed startling or novel. He spoke about the force of African nationalism. Of course. It was something that existed throughout the whole wide continent. He spoke quietly and logically about the need to come to terms with African nationalism as a political fact, and about the smallness of the world. Of course. After showing recognition of special problems arising from the large European population in various parts of that great continent who had no other home but Africa, he stated frankly, and as a friend of South Africa, Britain's policy in the areas of Africa for which the British Government bore responsibility. In a world divided between the Western Powers, Communist countries and the uncommitted nations it was, he said, Britain's task not only to raise living standards but to create societies where men could grow to their full stature. This must include the opportunity to enjoy an increasing share of political power and responsibility. Individual merit alone should be the criterion of a man's political or economic advancement. Though it was Britain's earnest desire to give South Africa support and encouragement as a fellow-member of the Commonwealth, there were some aspects of her policy which made it impossible for Britain to do this without being false to her own convictions.

There was at that time in Britain a boycott campaign against South African goods. After condemning the boycott campaign, Mr Macmillan concluded on the theme of the importance and fundamental strengths of the Commonwealth, which lay in flexible co-operation between independent countries pursuing common aims and purposes without obligation to agree on every subject. Present differences might be transitory: the friendship between Britain and South Africa was a legacy of history and belonged to those unborn.

All this was simply a restatement of British policy. Anyone who had expected Mr Macmillan to speak otherwise must have been totally unaware of his innate courage.

I have never been able to find out who produced the phrase 'Wind of Change' for that speech.

Soon after the African tour, not feeling very well, I took leave for a few weeks.

June 1, 1959

Dear John,

I tried to ring you up once or twice but was unlucky in finding you out. I do hope that you will have a little rest now. I am afraid that it is a long time since you had a holiday and you must

make sure not to overdo things. You know how grateful I am
to you for going on working with me when you have so many
other important commitments. I should hate to feel that this
was putting too great a burden on you. However, I dare say you
will find it easier working for Mr. Gaitskell.

Yours ever

HAROLD MACMILLAN

P.S. Give my love to Pamela. I hear she is back today.

June 2, 1959

My dear Prime Minister,

Thank you very much for your letter of June 1. It was very
kind of you to have found time to have written as you did. I was
much touched by what you wrote. I look forward to returning to
Downing Street with renewed vigour – if Tim and Tony and
Philip can stand it.

In the meantime Pamela has returned after hair-rising
experiences with her Bakhtiari tribesmen, including an en-
counter with wolves (she gave them one of her looks; exit wolf
pursued by a Pamela) but she enjoyed herself enormously; the
sun is shining and, after prodigious efforts I have at last
succeeded in busting the family trust in my favour and am now in
a position to be offensive to my creditors.

Yours ever,

JOHN

Pamela sends her love.

Then came the General Election of 1959, and the famous
Tory victory – the Tory glory, a majority of 100.

But we had our ups and downs during the campaign.
All election campaigns are tough. None is easy.

Mr Macmillan was in and out of cars and railway trains,
stumping the country. Now there was a great new test,
however – a test to which no political leader had yet been
really subjected : the test and trial of television. It was im-
perative that the Conservatives, and above all their leader,

the Prime Minister, should do well on TV. Through television Mr Macmillan was going to address himself directly to millions in their own homes. He *had* to shine.

But in the early part of the campaign the Conservatives had got themselves into a mess about their television broadcasts. The first of the broadcasts had gone badly. The broadcasts that followed were scarcely better. So it was decided that something special had better be done about the Prime Minister's final broadcast of the campaign. The next thing that happened was that I was prompted by Lord Poole, then deputy chairman of the party, and his Chief Publicity Officer, Ronald Simms, to seek out Mr Norman Collins, the novelist and television magnate. This I did. Would Norman Collins help to produce the Prime Minister's final election broadcast? Norman Collins said that he would not attempt the job unless he had seen the man in action beforehand. I replied that he could see the man in action in Nottingham tomorrow and insisted on taking him there myself.

Arrived in Nottingham, we went at once to the Prime Minister's meeting. It was much the same as every other big political meeting that I have been to : nice, honourable, respectable citizens were present, the great majority of them Conservative supporters. But Norman Collins remarked that the entrance of the Prime Minister was different in kind – he saw the soldier in him. Because Mr Macmillan was bolt upright and had his shoulders squared and knew how to pause long enough while the applause at his entry was still sounding, Collins realised that he was dealing with a man who understood his own value in public and how to make use of it. He straight away decided that the Prime Minister, to be shown at his true worth, should do his television broadcast standing up. He put this to Mr Macmillan later on. 'Oh, I see,' said Mr Macmillan, 'but am I allowed to?'

What impressed Collins about the Prime Minister's speech was that Mr Macmillan started on a deliberately low note; there was then a middle portion which was quite obviously the embodiment of a Conservative Research Department draft; but the peroration appeared to be entirely Mr Macmillan's own – and it was the peroration, not what had gone before, that made the speech. Collins had not previously met the Prime Minister. It was late in the evening when he did, in what, shall we say, was a family, rather than a fashionable, hotel. I took Collins up to a room from which Lady Dorothy – in a woolly dressing-gown – was just emerging, as nice and natural as usual but obviously preoccupied with the affairs of the tour. The room was in an awful state. There was a long table covered with papers, handbills, posters and election material presumably left by the agent. Ashtrays abounded, but none of them had been emptied. There were empty bottles and glasses about. The room was full of tobacco smoke.

We found Mr Macmillan quiet, calm and collected in this horrid scene, sitting in an armchair with his red boxes beside him. His first words to Collins were to say how deeply flattered he was that Collins – with characteristic politeness, Mr Macmillan insisted on behaving as though Collins were far the busier of the two – should have taken the trouble to come up to Nottingham at all. Then with a wave of his arm he indicated the room in all its campaign squalor and said how dreadful to think that the affairs of a great country were being conducted from a room like this.

Because he wanted to refer to notes during the vital broadcast, Mr Macmillan decided to speak from an upright reading desk which he, and he alone, believed had been

used by the younger Pitt. This, he thought, was somewhere in Downing Street. I could not find it, but a substi-
tute desk was produced. When it was shown to him the
Prime Minister said : 'Could I have something a little
higher, because when speaking one's arms rise so naturally,
you know ?'

We arranged for the broadcast to be rehearsed in the
ATV Foley Street studio, the smallest studio of Independent Television. It was there that Collins cheated out-
rageously. He said to the Prime Minister : 'This is going
so promisingly that there are only two things to be done
now. The first is that your voice is sounding hoarse and the
best medicine I know for a hoarse voice is port.' So the
Prime Minister had a glass of port. Well, that was all right.
But I began to get suspicious when Norman Collins made
his second point, which was that it was essential at a
rehearsal to time the broadcast exactly. The Prime Minister, his voice having been strengthened, went through the
broadcast and was exactly on time. Collins pronounced it
very good and congratulated him. The Prime Minister
said : 'I hope I shall be better when I do it live tonight.' By
now I had rumbled what Collins was up to. It was with the
B.B.C. however, and not with Norman Collins, that the
Prime Minister was supposed to make this important
broadcast. But Collins just said : 'Mr Macmillan, you have
already done it and you have been recorded.' Mr Macmillan
replied : 'You are a remarkable fellow. This is like going
to the dentist to have a tooth out and to be told that it has
already been drawn.'

When we told the B.B.C. that the broadcast had already
been done and would be delivered to them in a can, there was
a bit of a rumpus. The B.B.C. said that they had expected the
broadcast to be delivered live by the Prime Minister from

their premises. The Director-General's principal assistant, Mr Harman Grisewood, telephoned to say that the D.G. wished to speak to me. I – no doubt as a result of a bad line – thought that D.G. were the initials of someone whom I did not personally know. When this misunderstanding had been sorted out, it was made plain to the Director-General that the can, not Mr Macmillan, would be coming round. Mr Macmillan, however, with his usual courtesy said that nevertheless he would be present at the B.B.C. studios while his canned self was being broadcast. They were very nice to us and did us well with a cold buffet.

The broadcast was generally acclaimed as a resounding success. Even the *Daily Mirror* joined the Conservative Press in praising it as a real corker, and quite the best that had been delivered by a politician of any party.

During his last years as Prime Minister the Profumo affair did Mr Macmillan more harm than anything else in the whole of his administration, and it did a lasting damage to the Conservative Party. The handling of the incident suggested a lack of grip on the part of the Government and the nature of the incident suggested a lack of probity in high places. The British public may not be altogether scandalised or shocked by adultery, but they do dislike duplicity.

My own first knowledge of the affair began with a telephone call from Mr Mark Chapman-Walker, managing director of the *News of the World*, with whom I have had many adventures in war and peace. On this occasion, a winter night in 1963, he rang to ask if he could come round to our office at Admiralty House at once. He arrived within the hour.

What he had to tell me was the story going about Fleet

Street that John Profumo, the War Minister, had been carrying on with a girl who was also having an affair with a Soviet Naval Attaché. Her name, as it turned out, was Miss Christine Keeler, though he got it wrong at the time. I listened carefully to what Chapman-Walker had to say, and afterwards wrote it down. We then asked M.I.5 to send someone round. Someone duly arrived. From him we learnt that M.I.5 knew all about it. Profumo, he said, had certainly been in and out of Miss Keeler's place, and people in authority had warned Mr Profumo against the association. They were sure, however, that there had been no security risk.

Why, we asked the man from M.I.5, why had we not been told about this before? 'This is a free country,' he replied, 'not a police state.'

Stories continued to reach the Prime Minister's private office. We all know how it ended, after John Profumo's admission that he had lied to the House of Commons. His lie had been believed by his colleagues in the Government because his story was so incredible that it must be true. It was as simple as that. And anyone who scoffs at this explanation is not very wise in the ways of the world, because these things can and do happen. But I know one man who did not believe it at the time, and that was Enoch Powell.

The role of private secretary to a British Minister has always been a delicate one. Happily, however, no private secretary has ever been an *éminence grise*. Private secretaries in Britain are in a way a trade union, their mutual interest being to protect their masters. Their responsibility is nevertheless very great, particularly if they are professional civil servants. They are appointed as private secretaries because they are thought to be up-and-coming

Handshakes around the world

Wrestling in the Prime Minister's honour near New Delhi. Mr Macmillan's speech is safely in his Private

young men. If the Minister makes a mess of something, his private secretary should be sent for by the permanent head of the Department and asked in no uncertain terms how he let it come about. The private secretary should seek to protect his Minister at all times and also to run a two-way traffic in ideas, which means having the confidence not only of the Minister but of everybody else with whom he has business. With all of them he must be absolutely straight. Above all he must understand his Minister's mind. When the Minister has a 'bright idea' the private secretary should know instinctively how best to deal with it. The abler the Minister, the stronger the flow of 'bright ideas'. Nine out of ten of them may be impracticable. The tenth, if seized and acted upon, may turn out to be a masterstroke. It is very easy in a huge organisation to shoot down all ideas including the tenth. Yet the kind of man who keeps on throwing out ideas, even if nine-tenths of them are impracticable, is the kind of man to be cherished. This is where a good private secretary comes in. He touts the Minister's ideas around and with complete honesty he reports back on the reactions. He should know whose opinions the Minister particularly respects. Civil servants are, however, very polite in their doings with Ministers, but the private secretary, if he has established the proper degree of confidence with his master and the others, can cut a lot of cackle by saying in the privacy of the private office: 'All I can say to you, Minister, is that Sir George (or whoever it may be) says that it is absolute balls.'

When, on the other hand, Sir George comes up with one of *his* ideas, he might, if the private secretary is any good, try it out on him first. It is not for the private secretary to form any opinion of his own about the idea. It is for him, to the best of his ability, to advise Sir George about the likely

N

reaction. If he thinks that the Minister will not wear it at all, he should tell Sir George so, and then Sir George, if he still decides to put up his minute to the Minister, will know what is likely to happen. He could also suggest to Sir George a different way of approaching the Minister, which might result in a better reception for the idea. He should be the oil that greases the wheels and nothing more.

That has usually been the way with private secretaries in this country, unlike the Continent, where *chefs de cabinet* may be very important persons. In the old days here private secretaries were drawn from the younger sons of the gentility – young men who showed some promise. The Younger Pitt, for example, was at one time private secretary to James, Lord Lonsdale (1736–1802), whose political agent was Wordsworth's father. *That* must have been a pretty rum private office. Lord Lonsdale had nine pocket-boroughs and his Members were known as his Ninepins. He kept a dead woman in a glass-lidded coffin in his house and live wild horses in his park. He had a Whitehaven shopkeeper who had offended him pressed into the Navy and kept at sea for ten years. Off and on I worked in a Minister's private office for twenty years, but we never did anything like that.

Any Prime Minister is likely to find 10 Downing Street rather like the Vatican and himself cut off from outside gossip. A good private secretary should try to fill this deficiency.

The Younger Pitt when he was Prime Minister was told by his private secretary that in a Commons debate the previous night he was so drunk that his breath had given one of the clerks a headache. Pitt replied that he didn't want to hear any more about it : it suited him very well ; he had had the drink and the clerk had had the headache. The private secretary didn't mention it again. That is what I mean. A private secretary should be totally frank with his master, but he should never try to become an *éminence grise*.

Why did Bishop, Bligh and de Zulueta – three very promising public servants who could have expected to rise to the top – quit the Civil Service for private enterprise? Is it really true that in the public service it is still Buggins's turn? If not, why do so many of the best men leave?

I do not myself believe that it is now so simple as this. I do not believe that Buggins now gets his turn automatically when a top job is vacant. The best man for the job gets the job. But you are unlikely to be promoted over other people's heads until you are very near the top anyway. In the meantime Buggins – never having shown any great ability, but nevertheless moderately efficient, dependable and likeable – continues to hold jobs senior to yours, which you in your heart of hearts know that you could do better, until the time comes, after several years, when the post of permanent head of a great Department falls vacant. Then you may get it and Buggins not. But it is a long wait. It takes immense patience to put up with Buggins while he is a rung or two higher up the ladder than you are, and you know that you can do his job better than he can, particularly when you are getting tempting offers from outside.

Able and efficient though I believe most senior civil servants to be, not many get these tempting offers. The trouble is that those who do are probably the best. After all, there are not so many very highly-paid jobs available in private enterprise. Most senior civil servants would, I think, agree that their pay and conditions of service are all right.

To my mind two of the most fascinating – though possibly not the most commendable – earthly topics are women and power. Let us try to forget about the first and discuss power, which, the poet Milton said, 'erring men call chance'.

Mr Macmillan's attitude to power, I venture to say, is of some historical interest. I believe that from his youth up he always hankered after it. Yet he spent sixteen years in the political wilderness before he achieved office of any kind. His first office was merely that of Parliamentary Secretary at the Ministry of Supply in 1940; his second was not much grander – Parliamentary Under-Secretary of State at the Colonial Office.

He had always felt that his ability was better than most people's. Yet others with smaller minds had forged ahead and he had not. It would have broken a lesser man. But this one carried on despite pain from old war-wounds and many a disappointment thereafter.

He never sacrificed his principles. Although always a capitalist, Mr Macmillan insisted between the wars that the capitalist system would eventually rot unless it reformed itself. He told the Chancellor of the Exchequer (Neville Chamberlain) that the Government should intervene in the North of England to prevent further unemployment. The horror of unemployment haunted this kind man. At Westminster he was considered a clever but unpractical idealist. Conservative M.P.s scoffed at the midwife for a new world which stubbornly refused to be born. But it *was* born.

In sixteen years in the wilderness Mr Macmillan seemed

on account of his principles to be sacrificing any chances of power. In 1936 he said of the Tories : 'A party dominated by second-class brewers and company promoters – a Casino capitalism – is not likely to represent anybody but itself.' Naturally this offended some brewers and company promoters who, besides being Members of Parliament, thought that what they had been up to in their commercial affairs was not only in their own interest but also in the interest of the nation.

Mr Macmillan never abandoned his principles. Nor did he ever complain that his first offices were only those of Parliamentary Under-Secretary. When he was an Under-Secretary he revealed his inner feelings to me about power and himself just once. We were driving together in a car. After some desultory conversation he had relapsed into silence. Then he made a remark, almost to himself, which had nothing to do with what we had been talking about. He suddenly said with great force : 'I *know* I can do it.' He relapsed into silence again.

Suddenly he got power. He was appointed Minister Resident at Allied Force Headquarters in the Mediterranean. In a book about him, Anthony Sampson has recorded with percipient truth that Mr Macmillan's power there was 'colossal'. So it was, and he used it. Following him about in those days, I recall how brilliantly he disguised his power, however. Before he had done in the Mediterranean all of it was his bailiwick. I used to think in connection with his activity of the eighth verse of the Sixtieth Psalm : Italy was his wash-pot; over the Balkans he had cast his shoe.

I gained the impression from my earliest years with Mr Macmillan that he always wanted the power to match his ability. But kudos he seldom sought – give him the power and he would be perfectly content if others gained the credit.

By the end of the war in Europe he was, though few realised it at the time, Viceroy of the Mediterranean. American and British generals ate out of his hand.

All this was managed in a most extraordinary way, which was entirely Mr Macmillan's own. He had to play it down. There he was with offices in Algiers, Tunis, Naples, Rome, Athens, Bari, and so on. I might have secured some lovely places for him to live in, for example the Barberini Palace in Rome. But no, the rule was that we had to live simply. This we did.

Brilliance, a retiring nature, and great moral and physical courage have always impressed those who worked for him. He was the Viceroy of the Mediterranean by stealth.

Mr Macmillan managed things well, modestly and obliquely. The secret of his success was that he had the remarkable gift of inserting his guiding thoughts into other men's minds and making them think that the thoughts had all along been their own. He ran the whole show, but he was perfectly content to let the others think that they were doing so. So far as I know, he has himself revealed something of this only once, and that was in his book *The Blast of War*, in which he quoted from his diary of 5 July 1943: 'The Americans here ... are absolutely sound now. ... All I have to do is to follow in their footsteps, making polite noises of agreement with their ideas.' Despite the 765 pages of that splendid book, there is still a volume of hidden history behind those twenty-six words.

Power for power's sake was what he enjoyed. He has always been totally uninterested in the appurtenances and apparatus of power. When he was Prime Minister, he used to drive about in a very small, black, uncomfortable Humber car. I myself am of a sybaritic bent. I never ventured to argue with him about his choice of car, but he knew my feelings. When I was travelling with him in this awful black beetle, with my knees tucked under my chin, and a Chief of Staff, one of his minions, swept by in a huge black Rolls-Royce – or Sir William Haley, then the Editor of *The Times*, in a huge grey one – he would give me a quizzical, teasing look. His only concession to panache was that whenever he was really up against it he put on his Guards tie. Once a Grenadier, always a Grenadier.

CHAPTER SEVEN

Preserving Petworth

WITH the death of my Uncle Charles, the third Lord Leconfield, in April 1952, I inherited estates in Sussex, Cumberland, Yorkshire, Lancashire and Dumfriesshire amounting to 69,810 acres. He had himself inherited 110,000 acres – 66,200 in England and 43,800 in Ireland – which in 1883, according to *The Complete Peerage*, had produced an approximate yearly rental of £88,112. A handy sum to have, when you think how little fixed equipment a landlord had to provide in those days. My brilliant, able and erratic cousin George Wyndham did, however, manage to relieve Uncle Charles of the Irish property – though it may have been a blessed release, I suppose. I myself have parted with the Yorkshire, Lancashire and Dumfriesshire estates, to pay death duties, but have retained my land in Cumberland and 20,000 acres in Sussex.

My home in Cumberland is Cockermouth Castle, and the estate, which includes a great chunk of the Lake District, is mainly mineral, with iron ore and slate. I am fortunate in the fact that the slate, called Buttermere slate, is unique and is among the most attractive in the world. We are now trying to sell more of it abroad.

But my real home and centre is the Petworth estate in

Sussex, which is wholly agricultural, and the huge house that dominates it – surely one of the most beautiful white elephants in Europe, an immense white elephant adorned by one of the most splendid collections of pictures to be found outside a public gallery.

My ancestors' collecting mania lasted about three hundred years, beginning with the Percy acquisition of Van Dycks. We have thirteen of them, mostly acquired during Van Dyck's lifetime or shortly afterwards. It continued with the Duke of Somerset, then with the second and third Earls of Egremont. The third Earl, George, not only collected Old Masters but, as we have seen, he was a patron of many contemporary artists, the most notable being Turner, from whom he bought and commissioned twenty pictures. This same Lord Egremont's tastes also brought to Petworth many works by Reynolds, Gainsborough, Richard Wilson and other artists of his own and earlier periods as well as contemporary sculpture. The classical sculpture, some 85 pieces, was collected by the second Earl. It is mostly Roman, but the glory of this collection, known as 'The Leconfield Aphrodite', is Greek and attributed by the experts to Praxiteles.

When the Duke of Somerset married the Percy heiress and set about the rebuilding of Petworth he was determined to have the grandest possible house, worthy of his rank and wealth, and he employed the best men of his day for its embellishment, notably Grinling Gibbons, whose carvings cover the walls of one of the largest rooms. Miraculously, in spite of their profusion and elaboration, these carvings do not produce an effect of vulgarity or ostentation. I feel that Mr David Green in his splendid work on Grinling Gibbons hit on a happy simile when he likened this room to a symphony by Mozart.

The Duke of Somerset's grand staircase also lives up to its name, with walls and ceiling decorated by Louis Laguerre and now looking very splendid after recent restoration.

Outside, the second Earl added to my indebtedness to my ancestors by employing Capability Brown to landscape the park, with a result considered one of the most success-ful of his career. Its peace and dignity, embellished by the presence of the descendants of the herd of deer founded many centuries ago, is a perpetual joy.

All this was part of my inheritance from my Uncle Charles. But it was an inheritance that presented many difficulties and led to a long-drawn-out tussle with the Treasury. What happened was this. Before my uncle died I had pressed him to give Petworth and its park to the National Trust. I wanted to make sure that Petworth was preserved, and who could tell what the future might hold? I put this to Uncle Charles, and it was certainly one of the bravest things that I've ever done. He could have struck me out of his will. Happily he didn't. But when he died I was faced with heavy death duties. Petworth House (and the park but not the estate) had already been given to the National Trust with the huge endowment sum of £300,000. It now occurred to me that some of the 700 pictures in the house might also be handed over in lieu of death duty, to remain on the walls where they belonged as the property of the nation. My able solicitor and friend, Sir Leslie Farrer, was not very encouraging, but nevertheless I wrote to the Chancellor of the Exchequer :

My Dear Chancellor,
    I should be willing to consider offering to Her Majesty's Government, should the Government be prepared to consider receiving them in lieu of death duties (equivalent to their value)

on other properties, the great collection of pictures, Greek and Roman antiquities, the libraries and other treasures at Petworth.

There is no collection quite like it anywhere in the world today; and it oughtn't to be dispersed.

This suggestion is made without the knowledge of anybody except my Solicitor, Sir Leslie Farrer, and I therefore naturally want it to be treated as highly confidential. I do not know whether it involves a question of special legislation, as did the Duke of Wellington's offer about Apsley House seven years ago. In any case the circumstances are not the same. But I do feel that this chance is unique.

I should have liked to have had a word with you personally about this; but I hesitated to worry you at so busy a time. If, however, you could spare time for a word about it, I could of course come along whenever you liked.

Yours ever,

JOHN WYNDHAM

The Chancellor was kind enough to write back in his own hand :

My Dear John,

I am at once taking into consideration the imaginative offer contained in your letter of May 21st and of course I should wish to see you.

Owing to day and night on the Finance Bill I am leaving my friends here to arrange a meeting which might have to be after Whitsun.

Meanwhile all the best to you and your wife and how much we miss you.

I do hope to see the Collection.

Yours ever,

R. A. BUTLER

Presently I went to see the Chancellor, and it turned out that the Treasury had already been considering legislation to enable this sort of thing to be done. The next Budget provided it. Hot-headed and young, I immediately offered my best works of art to the Treasury. Oh, what a mistake! I was the guinea-pig for the new plan. The plan was all right in principle : the Treasury would take over the stuff in lieu of death duties and arrange for the National Trust to manage it. But the trouble and difficulty was in arriving at a fair price, for the Treasury had not been directly in the art market before. We had a terrible time. For example, what price to put on the Praxiteles Head of Aphrodite in the Beauty Room? The head was, of course, worth what it would fetch in the open market. But I was not selling in the open market : I was selling privately to the Treasury, and it was very difficult to decide the value – we couldn't look up the *Financial Times* to see what price Praxiteles heads were standing at today. And so it went on.

Various experts from Sotheby's, who were looking after me, the National Gallery, the National Portrait Gallery and the Tate Gallery met to discuss the subject at Somerset House. Sotheby's put up a very good fight – and a proper one too. But I was surprised at the way in which the people from the Galleries treated it all. We simply could not agree with them on prices. The representatives of the Galleries appeared to be quite unrealistic, and I and my advisers were constantly at odds with them. So was the Chairman of the National Trust, the Earl of Crawford and Balcarres, who wrote to Sir Edward Bridges, then permanent head of the Treasury :

10th February, 1956

Dear Bridges,

See enclosed from John Wyndham. Like the Ickworth letter I sent you it is personal to me : but none the less effective for that.

As you see, the difference between the 'official' valuation and his own is so great that, if the offer is final he will sell.

I make no comment on the valuation in detail; all I can say is that no one outside museum circles (and not many inside them) could conceivably regard a valuation made by a museum as comparable in accuracy with a Sotheby valuation. Long experience has shown me that few gallery officials have any knowledge of market prices of pictures : the V & A valuation of furniture at Petworth was made by an expert on Sculpture.

There are now two opposing valuations. It seems a pity that this situation has been allowed to arise. This new valuation is the first communication that Wyndham has ever received about the subject from any official source. This is surely the wrong approach (quite apart from bad manners). Surely the sensible approach would have been to discuss the valuation round the table with Wyndham, to see if Sotheby's had good evidence to support their figures, and to attempt to reach an agreement?

Agreement, by what has now happened, is obviously more difficult, especially as one valuation is 'official'. But would not the sensible thing, even now, be to get down at once to discussion with Wyndham? The alternative of a third valuation is possible : but unnecessary and an additional waste of time and money.

The second point, as you will see, is that the N.G. advises against accepting a number of pictures which Wyndham and the N.T. had agreed were appropriate for inclusion. These are the pictures we want : not all good pictures, but for one reason or another appropriate to Petworth. They are all hanging in the show rooms : they have all been placed there by Blunt.

The suggestion that they should not be included would absolutely wreck the house, leaving a series of spaces on the walls. The suggestion is quite lunatic, quite indefensible : quite exasperating.

No reasons are given. One can only assume that a 'Gallery' point of view has dominated – though even so the exclusions are wildly inconsistent. But we have all agreed that the 'Gallery' point of view was precisely what we wished to avoid : totally different criteria, we agreed, were applicable to country house collections. This has been the agreed basis of the whole conception. The N.G. list of exclusions is a complete negation of these principles. I think you will agree.

What is to be done to cut through this second muddle? Would not the best thing be for the N.T. to go carefully through our lists with Wyndham, and if we stand by them, then ask that they should be accepted? After all, we understand the N.T. point of view and he the Petworth tradition. Would not the result certainly be more sensible than the advice of someone who may know all about pictures, but knows nothing about Petworth or the N.T. – or apparently the basic principles on which we are all agreed these things are to be considered?

Cannot this be done? The only alternative would be for the N.G. and the N.T. to agree which pictures are to be included – under a Treasury Chairman – and this seems too ludicrous to contemplate.

I think that my two suggestions are the sensible way of dealing with the problems which need never have arisen. How much trouble would have been saved if it had been done months ago, instead of sending this sudden bombshell!

As I have said before, on the general question, administrative delays will sabotage the general idea. Owners won't face these obstacles and the years (three, I think in this case) of uncertainty and misery. The game is not worth the candle. If owners refuse to play – and if Wyndham sells – no one can blame them or the N.T.

All I hope is that, if Petworth can be saved, a less disheartening procedure will be followed in future cases. Otherwise I am afraid that the idea of preserving country houses and their contents is dead.

I am sorry to write like this : but after all you have done and I have tried to do, what could so easily and amicably have been arranged by good sense and consultation, has been reduced to confusion.

Yours ever,

CRAWFORD

And so the wrangle went on, month after month, until I received what proved to be a final letter from Sir Leslie Farrer:

October 2nd, 1956

Dear Wyndham,

I have now come back from my holiday and seen the correspondence from you in my absence and also your letter of yesterday to Burrell with its enclosure.

As I think you know I had a further interview with Bridges just before I left for my holiday and I arranged to see him again as soon as I came back. I rang up yesterday and shall be seeing him on Tuesday next, the 9th October, which was the earliest he could manage.

I have not hitherto given you any details of what has been happening for a variety of reasons, partly because some of it was confidential, partly because you were away anyway, and partly because I wanted, if I could, to see if things could get crystallised at the final interview, but I think I ought to tell you at once that my own mind is moving steadily in one direction and that is considerably reinforced by what I read in the various copy-letters you have sent me.

I know that this is going to be distasteful to you but what I do want you to do is to consider now very seriously whether it would not be wisest to accept the offer of £553,148 net which was made in the Summer, which has never yet been formally withdrawn and which Bridges, at my original interview with him, told me would not be withdrawn, although it was a mistake that it had ever been made.

My reasons for this feeling are these: it seems to me that there is no practical hope of getting the Treasury's Valuation increased by anything significant enough to matter. I will not go into my reasons for thinking that but I am satisfied of it now. There is also this Death Duty question. The difficulty over this, as you know, is that the Act is completely silent as to the price at which the Treasury are to buy and of course there is nothing to compel them to buy at all, and, therefore, there is nothing in law to prevent them saying the figure we offer is £x, which is smaller than our valuation because we have made a deduction for Estate Duty, and leaving you either to accept that offer or to reject it and sell elsewhere and pay the Duty.

What I myself am very much afraid of is this : if once we get to varying the list of Pictures which the Treasury are going to take over, and obviously their mind is moving very much in that direction, then the question of the offer for those particular things they do take becomes open once more and any offer they then make is bound to be only on the basis of a deduction for Estate Duty whereas, presuming we can still close for £553,148 that is a net offer and of course is equivalent to having sold the articles in question in the market for more than two and a half million pounds and paid the duty on them, plus the fact that they remain in the House.

I am, therefore, very anxious not to let matters drift into a position which gives the Treasury a reason for putting forward fresh figures because I think they are bound, in the way things have turned out, to be smaller.

Yours sincerely,

LESLIE FARRER

I had been hoping for a million pounds, but I took Sir Leslie's advice. Whatever may happen to me or my family, Petworth House, its contents and its park should be preserved for posterity. I am glad.

History has always echoed the sound of clogs going upstairs and the tinkle of tiaras coming downstairs. My family, despite a good many setbacks, have managed so far to stay on the landing.

Our roots are in land, and I have a great faith in the future of British agriculture. During the last war one of H.M. ships was moored alongside an American ship. A British sailor was doing something to the side of his ship,